ORGANIZATIONAL THEORY, NEW PAY, AND PUBLIC SECTOR TRANSFORMATIONS

Facilitating Strategic Change in Political Environments

Reginald Shareef

University Press of America,® Inc.
Lanham · New York · Oxford

Copyright © 2000 by
University Press of America,® Inc.
4720 Boston Way
Lanham, Maryland 20706

12 Hid's Copse Rd.
Cumnor Hill, Oxford OX2 9JJ

Library of Congress Cataloging-in-Publication Data

Shareef, Reginald, 1951-
Organizational theory, new pay, and public sector transformations :
facilitating strategic change in political environments / Reginald Shareef.
p.   cm
Includes index.
1.   Civil service—Salaries, etc. 2. Wage payment systems.
3. Organizational change. 4. Public administration. I. Title
JF1661 .S53   2000   352.4'7—dc21   00-064890 CIP

ISBN 0-7618-1849-9 (cloth : alk. paper)
ISBN 0-7618-1850-2 (pbk.: alk. paper)

⊖™ The paper used in this publication meets the minimum
requirements of American National Standard for Information
Sciences—Permanence of Paper for Printed Library Materials,
ANSI Z39.48—1984

To my wife Faye, and children
Malik and Amirah, for their
unconditional love and support

Contents

Preface

New Pay Transformations in Public Organizations

Reginald Shareef

The "private is better" approach to facilitating organizational change in public organizations has reached epidemic proportions. This is especially true concerning the use of variable or new pay processes to trigger strategic changes in public agencies. New pay concepts like Skill-Based Pay (SBP), gainsharing, and bonus pay are extremely popular in public change processes since it is believed they are the catalyst for cultural change, a learning organization, and enhanced productivity performance. These pay systems are thought to be superior to other pay innovations since they offer a direct link between pay and performance.

When these interventions fail, or create dysfunctions in the agency, many public administration theorists are quick to contend that these "alien" interventions are incompatible in public organizations solely for one reason -- they were imported from the private sector. This assertion is partly true. The various new pay change models used to transform public organizations were designed for profit-making enterprises. Consequently, these model's decision-making processes, goals, timetables, etc. "fit" with a business organization's environment but are incongruent with either the public agency's operating environment or value-orientation.

Failed new pay public sector change interventions also create negative political consequences. They waste taxpayer money, reduce organizational capabilities, and reinforce the perception of government ineptness. Internally, these unsuccessful efforts adversely affect the morale of public employees who often view these interventions as nothing more than costly, and passing, management fads.

But, as the old adage states, let's not throw the baby out with the bathwater -- new pay processes can work as effectively in facilitating public sector change as they have in private organizations. Three dynamics are required to bring this about: (1) a change model that is congruent with the public agency's environmental and value determinants; (2) identification of "best practices" that makes the

V

change model more praxis-oriented; and (3) identification of "dumb practices" that should be avoided in public change processes.

A consistent theme of this text stresses the importance of strategic vision and its link with vital organizational processes. New pay schemes often fail to meet their objectives because of poor or non-existent alignment between the strategic goal of the change process, the new pay concept(s) utilized, and timely redesign of supportive organizational subsystems. Because strategic pay (Lawler 1990) represents a behavioral-systems approach to change, emphasis is placed on the "fit" between these components (i.e., strategy and systems congruency) and new pay success.

In this context, Mohrman, Mohrman, and Tenkasi (1996, 6) write:

> Designers of macro systems design assume more malleability of organizational behavior than is actually the case. There is a great deal of evidence, for example, that reconfiguring work into cross-functional teams does not result in the intended collaborative behavior unless other aspects of the organization also change; behavior at the higher levels of the organization must also become collaborative, goal-setting and rewards of teams must be aligned, and other organizational systems must be reconfigured to fit a new collaborative way of doing work.

The alignment between these change components should be priority during the strategic planning process. Importantly, strategic planning must be holistic and inclusive. Roberts (1995a, 9) writes that, "A government agency needs a sound business strategy just as much as any business firm. If vision is dreams plus action, then strategy is the countless decisions that translate into a reality consistent and faithful to that vision. Strategic planning is something too important for just the planning department; everyone in authority and operations needs to be engaged, as well as the community".

However, strategy concerning new pay interventions is often segmented in planning or executive strategic committees and away from other management processes like human resource management and budgeting. Nothing could be more destructive to the new pay change process than this "walling off" practice (Kanter 1983). Because human beings bring different needs to the workplace, finding the right mix of incentives that produce the behaviors that then produce enhanced productivity is an iterate learning process for each agency. No programmed training package can replace this type of organizational learning.

Strategic alignment for public sector change, and unlike for business enterprises, must also be aligned with political processes like election cycles (Thurow 1980). It is politicians who fund these pay innovations. It is also lawmakers who expect to reap the political payoffs from the increased productivity outcomes that result from these pay interventions. Successful new pay processes provide politicians and elected officials with a campaign platform at reelection time.

New pay concepts like SBP also form the basis for creative public policy initiatives. For example, several writers (Roberts 1994; Thurow 1996) have suggested that the old social work contract of lifetime employment in public service be replaced with a new social contract -- lifetime employability. Such a contract would encourage the agency to invest in a lifetime of worker skill acquisition -- skills that will both (1) raise wages and (2) make the public worker marketable if the agency downsizes or outsources work. Obviously, legislators like the lifetime employability concept because of the organizational and political benefits it offers.

The text also addresses two related themes that will enhance the use of new pay concepts in agency change processes. Both themes are directed to public administration theorists and practitioners.

First, I have always been intrigued by the visceral reaction that many involved with the public administration enterprise have to management innovations that originate in the business sector. It is if these innovations are driven by "impersonal forces" rather than by human interpretations capable of shaping these concepts to meet agency objectives and values.

An underlying goal of this book is to promote the idea that human (1) interpretations and (2) reality constructions, and not impersonal forces with immutable characteristics, are the catalyst for organizational change (Silverman 1971). Thus, public stewards are ultimately responsible for the proper "fit" between new pay innovations and agency norms. Many of the examples used herein provide instances of public administrators fulfilling this institutional obligation. As we shall see, public administrators play dual roles, to insure fit, in new pay transformation processes -- that of leader (i.e., change agent) and daily operations manager.

Second, public administration scholars and practitioners have to develop better and more holistic relations with media representatives, especially those who write about organizations and management. As Chen and Meindl (1991) found, these writers disseminate information about changing organization performance (both public and private) and construct images (for public consumption) concerning management capabilities. Moreover, many of these writers possess an anti-deterministic ideology -- a belief that organizational leaders can positively impact the change process by influencing environmental determinants -- and tend to construct more favorable images of leaders/managers and organizations who share a similar ideology.

Many media representatives view public managers as deterministic concerning agency performance, primarily concerned with avoiding political embarrassment (Kaufman 1981). Consequently, when perspectives of public sector change are needed, it is most likely the opinions of business professors or consultants -- not public administration professors or managers -- that are sought.

The same phenomenon occurs when public organizations initiate strategic or macro change processes. They often hire business professors or consulting firms who are perceived as antideterministic but who either don't understand or value the "uniqueness" of public organizations. Much of this exclusion by government leaders is the result of the perceived deterministic bent of the field as a whole.

A better relationship between public administration scholars and managers with these writers will help public sector change for several reasons. The media, as opposed to markets, is often the catalyst for public sector change. Therefore, the views of theorists and practitioners with an antideterministic change perspective should be included by those in the business of leader/organization image construction.

An improved relationship with business writers will also enhance the inclusion of government employees and managers in the formative stages of strategic change planning. Currently, this group, along with public administration scholars, is largely ignored -- again, in favor of business leaders and professors (Roberts 1994). Part of the public stewardship role has to become the offsetting of this equilibrium imbalance.

The process of organization change offers those involved with utilizing new pay concepts an interesting paradox. Developing a strategic vision and implementing new pay is relatively easy but design alignment is an ongoing, trial and error process (Shareef 1997) that requires learning (and relearning) while doing (Morhman et al. 1996). Furthermore, this design strategy must also "fit" with political (re)election cycles and public policy initiatives.

The media represents a significant part of the public agency's turbulent environment. As such, there must be strategic alignment between the type of leader selected to facilitate agency change and the business press. Otherwise, that leader will not receive favorable image constructions by those who strongly influence public opinion.

Governmental decision-makers should be aware of these challenging issues when deciding to utilize new pay concepts in public sector transformations.

In the final analysis, this book seeks to provide politicians, managers, scholars, and interest groups with a broader perspective of public sector change and how new pay processes can successfully trigger successful transformations in these unique institutions.

Introduction

Something very disconcerting continues to occur in public sector change processes triggered by new pay interventions. Despite a growing body of empirical evidence that provides a conceptual framework for utilizing variable pay interventions in public organizations, the actual management practice appears to be dogmatic -- public leaders and consultants keep using popular business change models irrespective of the fact that they don't work in public organizations. Public leaders seem dogmatic and resistant to disconfirming evidence concerning the failure of these change policy processes (Sowell 1995).

So, as evidence mounts that popular business change models featuring new pay processes are not generic, and are inherently incongruent with the political environment and value-orientation of public organizations, many agency leaders continue to attempt to facilitate change based on high-involvement or high-performance change interventions. This is true of political leaders, especially governors, as well.

When these interventions fail, numerous reasons are offered as explanations. Some argue that because agency incentives emphasize security, workers and officials have learned to "sit tight" and wait out change efforts (Warick 1975). Similarly, others contend that since public organizations don't face issues of survival because of failed change efforts (Miller 1990), there is little incentive to change. Still others simply believe that interventions like new pay are "alien" to public organizations and are bound to fail (Wamsley, Goodsell, Rohr, Stivens, and Wolf 1987).

It is the hypothesis of this book that none of these assertions are accurate. Rather, new pay approaches have been ineffective in public sector cultural change and performance enhancement because of the inability of political and agency leaders to (1) recognize the uniqueness of public organizations and (2) adapt the high performance/new pay change model for congruency or "fit" with these unique characteristics.

Practically everyone -- theorists, consultants, practitioners -- overlooks the "uniqueness" of public organizations. Thus, generic organizational change models are often utilized to facilitate public sector transformations. It is now obvious that these generic change approaches will be successful in governmental agencies only if additional attention is paid to the legal and political operating environments of public organizations (Rainey 1992).

Numerous writers have highlighted the differences between public and private organizations (Lindblom 1977; Wamsley and Zald 1973).

However, there are also areas of convergence -- redesigned decision structures, theory Y notions of motivation, eliminating the dysfunctions of bureaucracy -- that overlap when new pay processes are used to trigger the transformations. New pay plans (i.e., the direct linkage of pay and performance) are often called "strategic pay" because of their impact on the redesign of all organization systems (Lawler 1990).

Perry and Kraemer (1991, 8) have also been concerned about the inattentiveness that generic organizational theory pays to public administration values:

> If the administrative route were selected as the sole perspective of public administration, could we continue to speak of "public administration?" ... would profit conscious business school types appreciate the value of the public interest as an important aspect of administrative science?

These writers view public administration as a special management activity. Consequently, their writings helped evolve the "public management" paradigm that merged generic organizational theory concepts involving knowledge, techniques, and skills with unique public administration activities like public interest values, public goods, and social affairs.

Roberts' (1995a; 1995b) High Performance Government (HPG) change model represents a "fit" between classical organization theory and the public management paradigm. Generic organizational theory concepts involved in the HPG model are leadership, vision and values, and the strategic alignment of systems and structures. This alignment includes new pay systems.

In this respect, her change model is similar to Lawler's (1986; 1992) high-involvement and Pfeffer's (1998) high-performance change models that were designed for business organizations.

However, Roberts (1995a, 2) argues that the HPG is a unique public sector change model, distinguished from other public and private change interventions. She writes:

> We go far beyond reinventing government and total quality management advocates who assume that borrowing private-level prescriptions are enough (e.g., government should introduce competition, be entrepreneurial, customer-driven and market oriented). Government and public service should not be pale imitations of private enterprise, or they will fall far short of delivering what our communities and free enterprise need.

The HPG change model is designed based on the political culture of public organizations as opposed to the market-driven environments

XI

of private enterprises. For example, Roberts (1995b) advocates the use of parallel structures as crucial decision-making mechanisms during public organizational change. These parallel structures are required to make sure that legally-mandated public services are provided -- even during organizational transformation.

Conversely, Lawler (1998) sees little need for parallel structures during change in private sector businesses. Ledford (1998) views them as absolutely destructive to the change process. The reason for differences between the Roberts' and Lawler/Ledford position on parallel structures -- the political and legal operating context of public organizations.

Industrial Democracy, Public Agencies, and New Pay

The early 20th century political reformer Herbert Croly called for a scientific public administration that facilitated democratization throughout all aspects of American life (Pearson 1998). As this call relates to institutional life, democratization can only be manifested through a shift from autocratic to participative, high-involvement work cultures. A number of public administration theorists still refer to these shifts as transformations to industrial democracy (Starling 1986).

It is important to note that the research shows that new pay interventions are only successful in high-involvement, not bureaucratic, work cultures.

Roberts (1995a) sees a linkage between democracy and high-performance government. She notes a basic contradiction between democratic processes and the anti-democratic ways of bureaucracy. She also calls for a paradigm shift from exploitative/benevolent autocratic management systems to consultative/participating systems for governmental agencies seeking to improve performance. Others have also reported that the lack of democracy/participation in public organizations is a societal and organizational contradiction (Shareef 1990).

The academic fields of humanistic psychology and organization theory/design have been active in the democratization of the workplace for the past 50 years. The goal has been the creation of participative work cultures and a better understanding of the relationship between strategy, organization design and behavior, and productivity. Employee involvement is crucial in the continual alignment between strategic pay and high performance government.

High-involvement organizations offer the best example of total workplace democratization. Huse and Cummings (1989, 267) describe these organizations by stating, "Almost all features of the organization are designed to jointly promote high levels of involvement and performance, including structure, work design, information and control systems, physical layout, personnel policies, and reward systems."

Workplace democratization is the centerpiece of new pay interventions in public organizations. Industrial democracy or high-involvement culture is the seamless variable that runs through strategic pay interventions and are an integral component of new pay plans designed to enhance performance. In fact, the ultimate success or failure of these pay interventions in governmental agencies will be determined by how "deep" democratization/participative management is allowed to penetrate traditionally bureaucratic public institutions. Poor strategic alignment of the new pay intervention with supportive (1) organizational subsystem redesign and (2) political processes are reasons most public sector change interventions have failed.

Overview of the Book

New pay concepts do not inherently undermine traditional public administration values. As we shall see later, these new pay strategies "fit" well with unique public administration activities, especially public service motivations.

Chapter I reviews the evolution of the new pay change model and specifically how it causes dysfunctions in public organizations. A discussion of how the new pay model can be adapted for congruency with public administration values, motivations, and political operating environment is then discussed. Next, a change model that recognizes the uniqueness of public agency transformation is presented.

The second chapter outlines and discusses seven best practices of public agencies that have created "fit" between new pay approaches and strategic change objectives. Several of those "best practices" focus on the management of the turbulent political environments of public organizations while others deal with the key issue of strategic alignment between new pay processes and agency objectives. Still other practices are concerned with the design of successful new pay interventions.

Chapter III reviews seven deadly practices that are fatal to variable pay efforts in the public sector. Some are obvious, others are not. Regardless, failure to avoid these habits will undermine the best-designed and well-intentional new pay intervention. Like the list of best practices, these habits to-be-avoided fall into three related categories -- the political operating environment of public organizations, strategic alignment, and design issues.

Chapter IV explores the issue of exactly where the new pay intervention should begin -- with workers or management. This is a much discussed topic among those involved with the organization change process in general. While there appears to be no absolute correct answer to this question, (1) the size of the agency and (2) how quickly it can diffuse the pay innovation to the other group are crucial determinants in deciding exactly where to start strategic pay interventions.

Chapter V discusses why it is important for public administration theorists and practitioners to improve relations with an important environmental stakeholder -- the business press. Currently, that relationship is poor because media elites tend to view the field of public administration as deterministic and its leaders not believing that direct actions can positively influence agency outcomes. These press attitudes shape public perceptions about the public administration enterprise. Moreover, these impressions lead to the exclusion of the field's scholars and practitioners from strategic planning concerning new pay interventions. It also leads to the irreplaceable loss of their expertise -- especially concerning the political dynamics of public sector change -- from the transformation process.

Chapter VI outlines the relationship between new pay processes and organization learning. Some of these interventions (e.g., skill-based and competency-based pay) are directly linked to the organizational learning process through skills acquisition. Conversely, gainsharing and bonus pay plans are tied to a broader set of learning activities that fall under the rubric of "business education". Regardless, all new pay interventions constitute "double loop" learning processes where organizational subsystems (particularly training) have to be redesigned to enhance skill and/or business knowledge attainment.

The final chapter offers thoughts, ideas, and recommendations about the future of new pay interventions in public organizations.

Chapter 1

New Pay Practices and Public Sector Change

Public organizations, at every level, are currently involved in strategic organizational change and redesign processes. Known by various names -- reinventing government, high-involvement management, high performance management -- these change processes are designed to create participative work cultures, enhance teamwork, facilitate organization learning, and improve productivity outcomes. In effect, these reforms seek the fundamental redesign of governmental institutions (especially the civil service) (Ingraham and Romzek 1994) and enhanced efficiency and customer service (Roberts 1994).

Like their private sector counterparts, public agencies face profound challenges in the twenty-first century. These challenges do not appear to be directed at the institution of government itself but rather are focused on the often poor organizational performance by public organizations (Posner and Rothstein 1994). One of the more innovative ways that public agencies have utilized to confront these performance challenges has been the use of new or variable pay plans, in conjunction with high involvement or high performance change models, to trigger organization transformation.

"New pay" is a total compensation strategy that targets pay programs at performance goals the organization wants to accomplish (Lawler 1984). Variable pay schemes are thought to be superior to other performance-enhancing change interventions since they offer direct linkage between pay and performance. The new pay concept serves government change processes by triggering organization redesign and facilitating a shift from hierarchical, theory X, mechanistic management to flatter, theory Y, organic organizational cultures. This represents a shift from segmentalistic (i.e., anti-change and hostile to innovation) structures to more integrative entities that "combine ideas from unconnected sources. ... And see problems as wholes, related to larger wholes, thus challenging established practices" (Kanter 1983, 29). This type of paradigmatic cultural shift is a fundamental goal of strategic change processes in public organizations.

A recent variable pay change intervention provides a good example of a local government linking pay and performance while responding to an organizational challenge. As part of its strategic plan, the City of Charlottesville, Virginia desired to reduce the number of position classifications. All city employees were involved in the rewriting of job classifications, which were reduced from 270 to 100. Variable pay options like team bonuses and gainsharing were institutionalized throughout the organization to reward employees directly for their redesign efforts and the cost savings that resulted from those efforts (Roberts 1995a).

Variable pay plans are also being used in public agencies as recruitment and retention tools. Often, public employees leave government service because of low pay. New pay schemes allow government entities to pay more for individuals who possess needed skills/attributes or to structure reward systems to compensate employees for learning desired skills/behaviors.

Several years ago, I served as a consultant to a municipal police department. The agency was attempting to recruit and retain more minority officers. Low starting pay was seen as a barrier to accomplishing this strategic objective. A secondary goal was a better-educated police force. Paying educational expenses for officers to complete 2 or 4 year degrees (i.e., indirect pay) was viewed as a viable option for the recruitment and retention issue. There were also discussions about using Skill-Base Pay (SBP), combined with base pay, for officers who volunteered for community policing activities or mounted patrols (Shareef 1994a).

There are three components of this total compensation system (Schuster and Zingheim 1992, XVI):

- Base Pay - Under new pay, base pay levels are matched as closely as possible to the competitive labor market, allowing the organization to obtain quality talent. Base pay can be adjusted from the competitive market to emphasize jobs and skills that are strategically important to the organization. Base pay serves as a platform for variable pay.

- Variable Pay - The centerpiece of new pay is variable pay. Variable pay, in forms such as group variable pay, business plan gainsharing, winsharing, lump-sum awards, and individual variable pay, has the flexibility needed to match dynamic circumstances. Variable pay for broad employee populations is able to respond to changes and complex challenges that employees face.

- Indirect Pay - Flexible benefit planning was an early move to new pay. However, many organizations offer benefit choices only to match what other organizations do, rather than to aid performance and emphasize goals.

Schuster and Zingheim (1992, XI) wrote the first definitive book on new pay and described the concept in the following manner:

Pay programs are visible and powerful communications of organizational goals, priorities, and values. Proper alignment with what is to be accomplished is essential. We believe that new pay emphasizes solutions that reflect the proper organizational direction and omits those practices that are counterproductive. ... Many top-performing organizations moved to more flexible and responsive pay strategies that matched the circumstances in which the organizations found themselves. The rejection of "one size fits all" traditional pay practices gave birth to the new pay.

The new pay concept suggests that these pay innovations are permanent rather than a passing fad. Indeed, Edward Lawler of the University of Southern California School of Business originated the "new pay" term and linked it to values and processes that he called "The New American Management" (1984). As such, the concept fits best with several redesign components including decentralization, institutional based rewards for performance, and congruency between pay and strategic goals.

New pay plans (i.e. the clear linkage of pay and performance) like Skill-Based Pay (SBP) and gainsharing are strategic change interventions that must be aligned with redesigned subsystems to facilitate transformations and enhance effectiveness. The linkages between new compensation schemes and performance are often called "strategic pay" because of their impact on the design of all organization systems. Human resource, information, and financial measurement/valuation systems are key subsystems that influence behavior and must be realigned as an organization changes forms (Mohrman et al. 1996).

Fundamentally, new pay strategies seek to establish a direct relationship between employee/organizational performance and rewards. These pay plans are also designed to meet business and human resource challenges, thereby enhancing performance. For example, if the strategic goal is to create a learning organization, SBP or competency-based pay (pay for knowledge) would be an appropriate pay intervention. On the other hand, if the strategy calls for productivity increases, bonus pay or gainsharing are pay systems that can be tied to performance.

This management approach has been most successfully implemented in business organizations that sought to create what are known as high-involvement (Lawler 1986) or high-performance (Pfeffer 1998) work cultures. In these organizations, employees have significant input in the redesign of the enterprise's various subsystems, especially reward and performance. Here, both workers and management possess knowledge of the determinants of organizational effectiveness and a knowledge of pay alternatives that enhance performance.

The underlying "rewarding" philosophy in these organizations is that although individuals have differing compensation goals, they have access to all benefits in the organization if they desire and put forth the effort.

New pay processes form the integral component for the high involvement/high performance change model(s). The motivational bases of this change model are premised on the utilitarian theory that workers will increase performance if there exists a clear link between pay and productivity outcomes. Private sector firms like Proctor and Gamble, Monsanto, General Mills, and Allied Signal have all successfully utilized new pay concepts as catalysts for organizational transformation.

The new pay/high-involvement approach also provides the conceptual change model that large consulting firms like PricewaterhouseCoopers (PwC) use when facilitating cultural and performance changes in public organizations. And ... therein lies a fundamental problem for public agencies wanting to use new pay schemes to trigger change.

The High-Involvement/Performance Model, Strategic Change, and Agency Dysfunctions

While the new pay/high-involvement model works well for profit-making businesses, it creates dysfunctions when implemented in the political, legal, and cultural operating environment of public organizations. A recent example will clarify this point. The Virginia Department of Transportation (VDOT) used this change model with Skill-Based Pay (SBP) the lead change variable. The strategic objectives of this transformative endeavor was the creation of (1) a participative culture, (2) a learning organization, and (3) multi-skilled workteams.

Because SBP only works in a participative or high-involvement culture (Shareef 1998), organizations have to maintain dual compensation systems -- the traditional classification and the new pay system -- until a majority of workers voluntarily transfer into the variable pay plan.

SPB was designed to be implemented in VDOT through a series of long-term phases or pilot programs. The process began in late 1993 with Phase 1. In-house surveys conducted during the 1994-95 period indicated that workers were overwhelmingly satisfied with all relevant issues associated with SBP. Based on these results, the pay intervention was expanded in December 1995 to cover a pilot population of 509 employees or 18% of VDOT's maintenance workers.

However, in early 1996, SBP participation became mandatory. VDOT officials and the consulting group determined that the administrative costs of maintaining dual compensation systems was too expensive. This type of unilateral decision may have been acceptable, because of competitive pressures, in a business enterprise. In a public organization, because of political considerations and a culture that values fairness, the decision was disasterous:

> The lack of employee involvement in the discussion concerning participation, coupled with a top-down mandate to eliminate dual compensation systems, has severely threatened the future success of the program. Both VDOT officials and several state legislators revealed, for example, that because of forced participation, an employee telephone "hot line" to various state lawmakers had to be established to handle worker complaints and concerns (Shareef 1998, 16).

The political fallout from the dismantling of the dual pay systems continues to haunt agency planners and consultants. Because of worker/constituency complaints, state lawmakers have been reluctant to provide additional funding for advanced phases of the process. A PricewaterhouseCoopers (PwC) consultant associated with the change effort recently admitted that the agency had a difficult time getting money from the 1999 General Assembly for the competency-based management phase. Competency-based management is a form of SBP that pays managers for mastering desired organizational competencies.

These dysfunctions did not occur as a result of bad intentions on the part of VDOT leaders or PwC consultants (although many VDOT workers now believe that the goal of the SBP intervention was a linear plan to (1) raise their pay rates higher than those of their private sector counterparts, (2) then outsource their work because it would be cheaper, and (3) consequently, downsize the agency). Rather, these dysfunctions occurred because the high-involvement/performance model was developed for profit-making businesses and not political entities.

In fact, the decision to abandon the dual classification system after two years was predictable since proponents of the model contend that full implementation and diffusion of new pay processes should occur within two years (Ledford 1998). They also strongly discourage the use of pilot programs.

Because the model was designed based on the competitive economic contingencies and (shorter) time horizons of private enterprises, and not the political/legal contingencies and longer-time horizons of public institutions (Thurow 1996), the new pay/high-involvement change approach was incongruent with both the public organization's operating environment and value-orientation.

New Pay and Public Service Values

The high-involvement model, because of its focus on bottom-line efficiencies, also undermines traditional public administration values like the public interest and public service. When business professors write about new pay, they usually do so from a purely utilitarian perspective (Perry 1994). Most public administration theorists reject this utilitarian approach for public organizations because it is indifferent to public service motivations. Clearly, new pay systems used in public sector transformations must be congruent with the basic extrinsic needs of employees while promoting public service values.

While the profit-motive is the underlying value that drives the high-involvement model, public interest and public service motives will give structure/design to new pay change processes in the public sector. This was demonstrated in Norfolk, Virginia where that city's political leadership sought to transform the bureaucratic culture. However, they realized that simultaneous and radical systems change, known as organizational frame-bending by business theorists (Nadler and Tushman 1989), would adversely affect ongoing service delivery and management (Roberts 1995b).

Consequently, parallel structures were created wherein managers met and planned the change process while also managing the everyday task operations of the municipality. The managers essentially walked between two contradictory worlds -- the world of change agents and the world of bureaucrats. Moreover, the parallel structures were not temporary. They would remain until a participative culture was diffused throughout city government. This type of gradualism, and the use of additional structural mechanisms, is found in public sector change processes and are necessary for the continuity of legally-mandated service delivery, efficient public management, and ease of cultural transformation.

However, this is not the case with business entities because of the competitive pressures they face. These pressures demand speed and flexibility. Pay and performance systems have to be fluid to be congruent with the fluidity of the modern business organization's turbulent operating environment.

Parallel structures hamper the business organization's response to its highly competitive environment. Thus, they are not part of the high-involvement of high-performance change model. Conversely, parallel structures are an integral component of public sector change because of the dynamics of operating in a political/legal environment grounded in public interest and public service values.

Both public and private organizations operate in turbulent, however vastly different, environments. Agencies obtain revenues from appropriations while enterprises are rewarded or penalized because of market performance. Governmental agencies often have a diversity of missions, with an emphasis on fairness and impartiality, while enterprises possess a single goal -- profit-making. Strategic changes in public organizations are generated by legislators, voters, the media, and/or interest groups, while changes in business enterprises are triggered by desires for competitive advantage.

As such, the change model developed for private businesses is not sensitive to either the political environments or values of public agencies. Often, public managers realize this only after proposing a new pay solution to an environmental challenge. Several years ago, a public school district in a southern state attempted to alleviate its shortage of minority teachers by offering a signing bonus.

While there was a clear linkage between pay and the strategic goal, the plan was abandoned after the teachers' union declared the plan unfair to non-minority members. The school board and local media representatives agreed. It is interesting to note that if this plan had been proposed in a business enterprise, and would have enhanced the strategic goal of diversity, no reversal of policy would have taken place. Efficiency, not perceived unfairness, would have been the determining value.

Public Service Work Motivations

The high-involvement/high-performance model is also incongruent with public service motivations because of its utilitarian perspective. This perspective suggests that workers are motivated solely through pay, benefits, and career opportunities. Thus, the model is completely indifferent to public service motivations -- an individual's predisposition to respond to motives grounded uniquely in public organizations (Perry 1994).

These public service motivations often fall into two categories – norm-based and affective. Norm-based motives are actions generated by values like civic duty and the public interest. Affective motives are behavioral triggers that link emotional responses like compassion and self-sacrifice to various social contexts. It is believed that these public service motives are more likely than purely utilitarian motives to build employee commitment in governmental organizations because of their value-orientations.

Because of these incongruencies with the political environment and values of public organizations, the high-involvement/high-performance change models should not be utilized by public agencies to trigger strategic change. What is needed is a change model that incorporates high-performance processes with unique public administration (1) political/legal determinants, (2) values, and (3) motivations.

Robert's High Performance Government Change Model

Professor Deborah Roberts, of the University of Virginia's Cooper Center for Public Service, has designed a change model specifically for public organizations. Popular with local governments in Virginia, the High Performance Government (HPG) model offers a sharp dichotomy on the roles of public and private managers during the change process:

> We do not in anyway diminish the public thrust. ... public managers have always had an added charge that private managers do not face: accountability to citizen owners, rooted in rule of law and due process (Roberts 1995a, 2).

Roberts' model emphasizes the development of a participative culture and discusses shifts in four areas designed to achieve systemic, system-wide transformation. These four change levels are:

- Leadership: Shared leadership roles between top administrators – administrators are both leaders and managers who are responsible for strategic visioning/valuing. They are also the facilitators of systems integration.

- Vision and Values: Public employees need to make their jobs value-rich; consequently, each employee should articulate a personal vision about what means the most to them and how it is connected to their work.

- Strategy, Structures, and Systems: Strategic planning should include everyone in line authority and operations, as well as members of the community; major support systems -- human resources, financial systems, budgeting, etc. need to be revamped; and structures can be consolidated to share administrative services for greater coordination and efficiency.

- Capacity Building: Creation of a learning government, teamwork, and community building.

The HPG model provides an outline of organizational and political processes necessary to facilitate change in governmental institutions. Designed for a democratic and pluralistic society, HPG offers a set of "communitarian values" that provides a holistic framework for public administrators and community groups to jointly facilitate change. The model, while sharing organizational theories of leadership behavior and worker motivation/satisfaction with Lawler's high-involvement and Pfeffer's high-performance models, is uniquely suited for public organizations because of involvement by government's true owners -- the citizens. The HPG approach also recognizes the political dynamics that help determine the success of high performance interventions.

From a new pay perspective, the HPG framework suggests that incentives for productivity be built into the budgeting process. Pay and performance are linked with community input becoming a powerful determinant in the compensation process. For instance, Hampton, Virginia does annual citizen satisfaction surveys of its services with employee pay tied to survey results (Roberts 1995a).

Implications

Several change models are commonly used to trigger strategic transformations in public organizations. Developed for, and successfully implemented in many business enterprises, these change models feature new pay processes like SBP or bonus pay as the lead change variable. However, when utilized in public organizations, these models inevitably produce dysfunctional outcomes because of incongruencies with the political/legal environment and value-orientations of public agencies.

Roberts' HPG model, designed specifically for public organizations, does "fit" with the environment and values of governmental institutions. Used extensively in local governments, the model provides an effective change framework for state and federal agencies as well. While the HPG model offers a functional approach for implementing change, it seems a complementary list of high-performance best practices that go beyond issues of philosophy, architecture, and world-view -- all found in the HPG model -- should be presented.

These management practices need to be internally aligned with both the values of public administration and the (new pay) strategic goals of the agency. Externally, they must be consistent with the political operating environment of the public organization. These "best practices" provide a more praxis-understanding for public managers who are either using the HPG model to implement variable pay plans or who are considering these pay interventions.

In Chapter 2, I distill from various studies, literature, personal observations, and experiences seven "best practices" that have successfully been used to implement and diffuse new pay processes in public agencies. All are congruent with the HPG model. Several of the practices, for example the inclusion of public administration scholars and public managers on initial strategic planning committees and joint labor-management collaboration, are actually antecedents of the change endeavor. Others, like team-based pay and alignment between pay and strategic goals, are functional processes that will enhance the efficacy of the HPG as a change intervention.

Chapter 2

Seven New Pay Implementation Practices For Public Agencies

In the previous chapter, we reviewed the dynamics of the new pay concept as a change intervention, why strategic change in public organizations is unique, and how new pay processes "fit" with the architecture of Roberts' High Performance Model (HPG).

This chapter will present seven practices that have been used in various public agency change interventions featuring new pay. Although some of the processes deal with internal management processes, while others are concerned with external political determinants, all are aligned or consistent with (1) the architecture of the HPG change model and (2) new pay dynamics.

These seven practices are:

- Executive Leadership

- Managing the Zero-Sum Politics of Public Sector Change

- Providing Quality Customer Service

- Aligning Strategy, Pay, and Performance

- Designing Team Based Compensation Systems

- Regulating the Speed of Change

- Utilizing Multiple New Pay Plans Simultaneously

Executive Leadership

The role of leadership as a catalyst for organizational change is well-documented in the literature (Bennis and Nanus 1985; Tichy and Ulrich 1984). One leadership change strategy, transformational leadership, suggests that leaders must be visionary and inspire their followers to make the necessary changes to make the vision a reality (Bennis and Nanus 1985). Importantly, transformational leadership is an appropriate trigger for using new pay processes in the public sector (Perry 1994).

Public sector executives seem to especially utilize the transforming leadership principles of (1) vision creation, (2) reinforcing the rationale for change, and (3) delegation of authority. In 1996, the United States Postal Service (USPS) implemented a change process designed to improve customer service, enhance agency efficiency, and improve financial performance. Bonus pay for meeting specified targets was implemented for the managerial group.

The "instrumental leadership" concept links the vision/charisma of the leader to the redesign of the organization's various subsystems (Nadler and Tushman 1990). The intent here is consistent with the strategy of shaping congruent behaviors in support of the organization's strategic vision. Going a step beyond transformational leadership, the instrumental approach encourages the leader to be actively involved in creating the "fit" between strategic vision, redesigned subsystems, and performance outcomes.

This type of change process was initiated in the USPS by then Postmaster General Marvin Runyon. He articulated a vision of the USPS becoming "The premier provider of Postal Communications in the Twenty-First Century" (United States Postal Service Publication F-6 1997). PMG Runyon's rationale for the change process -- "meeting the challenge of an increasingly competitive environment." He also redesigned the training, appraisal, and reward system for the managerial group to be congruent with the agency's strategic goal.

The decentralization of power is a hallmark of all high performance systems. It signifies that the transformational leader has pushed leadership tasks down into the organization. In the USPS' new pay change process, for instance, PMG Runyon empowered Finance Director Michael Riley to lead/manage the change intervention. This type of delegation has been called "the power dynamics shift from control to commitment and empowerment" (Roberts 1995a, 7).

Sometimes delegation of new pay processes results in greater self-management or self-regulation. After becoming Governor of Virginia in 1994, George Allen decentralized decision-making for the state's colleges and universities. Since then, winsharing has been administrated in a near laizze-manner.

In the Virginia's system of higher education, winsharing provides non-monetary rewards for academic departments that come in under budget (with no diminishment of service or productivity). This pay concept is similar to gainsharing except there are no monetary bonuses. In a typical winsharing payment plan, remaining budgetary funds are divided equally among department members who spend their "winshare" at their discretion.

I have seen funds spent on computers and computer software, professional travel, research projects, dues for professional organizations, and purchases of copiers. Faculty members may give their share to another member if they desire. Originally intended as a temporary measure to offset modest annual salary increases, winsharing (because of its popularity among faculty) is now viewed as a tax-free component of a faculty member's total compensation package.

Administrative controls insure that none of the funds are used as salary increments. Otherwise, it is totally left to the faculty member's discretion, and definition of professional development, as to how the funds are used. It is easy to see how this new pay process triggered employee involvement and empowerment for the state's faculty members concerning efficiency and professional development.

In the HPG model, managers throughout the institution have to provide leadership while assuming that the basic functions of the organization are performed well. This is also true in Lawler's (1992) high-performance management model but the leadership/management continuum is more acute in public organizations: ... "elected policymakers choose professional city managers, county administrators, and town managers to run the organization. They in turn hire department heads. These top administrators see that the whole comes together: they have a dual role of both management and leadership" (Roberts 1995a, 7).

This leadership/management duality is a prominent practice in public organizations that have successfully implemented strategic pay. The USPS' variable pay plan is both lead and managed by Michael J. Riley, the Postal Services' Budget Manager. The leaders/managers of SBP in VDOT and gainsharing in Baltimore County are found in the HRM Departments. The "Deans" of the various colleges in Virginia's Higher Education administer winsharing.

All of these leaders/managers deliver information, knowledge, power, and rewards to facilitate organization change processes. They also help redesign systems, create new organizational identities (Shareef 1991), and "make sense" (Weick 1995) out of new pay processes for workers, taxpayers, and legislators. These leader/managers (along with policy makers and senior managers) constitute the executive leadership teams in public agencies.

These teams offer direction for the intervention, visit implementation sites and interview employees, and provide feedback to lower-level managers on alignment issues. Their offices also serve as technical and information centers. In the successful agencies surveyed, these executive teams/technical centers were integral components of the change intervention.

Managing the Zero-Sum Politics
of Public Sector Change

Our political system is characterized by politicians seeking reelection every two, four, or six years. Long-term projects, like strategic pay processes, involve long periods when costs accrue with the benefits often coming after the politician has left office. Therefore, lawmakers are more interested in short-term projects that bring them votes (Thurow 1980).

Pilot programs and gradual implementation of new pay processes allow politicians to campaign for reelection on improved governmental performance. This usually insures continued funding for the project. Obviously, private sector managers are not concerned with these types of political issues.

Public administrators involved in strategic change must be aware of this political dynamic. The election year cycle allows public change agents to gear strategic management processes, especially performance assessment and budget requests, for congruence with relevant political cycles. This insures continued political support for the change effort.

A significant portion of the Virginia Department of Transportation (VDOT) strategic thinking focuses on results that deliver for state politicians:

> VDOT's vision sets the stage for strategic direction and activity for
> a four to six year period. VDOT determined this time-frame based
> on the election cycle in Virginia. VDOT management prefers to be
> prepared to propose their thoughts on the Department's direction to
> a new administration before election day. This direction is

budgeted, implemented, and measured from year to year. Adjustments are made as required (Sorrell and Lewis 1998, 6).

In Baltimore County, Maryland Executive C.A. Ruppersberger is both an executive leader and elected official. In 1994, he campaigned on a platform of making government more efficient and effective through the use of the gainsharing incentive program. Since his election, the program has been so successful it has been (1) touted as a model gainshare program for public organizations, (2) listed on the front page of the Wall Street Journal, and (3) featured as a case study in a prominent public administration publication.

In addition, the gainshare program has served as the catalyst for a second new pay program in Baltimore County -- SBP. Needless to say, Mr. Ruppersberger's campaign in the year 2000 will highlight the efficiency accomplishments of gainsharing. Here, performance assessment of a new pay intervention are expected to result in political payoffs.

Mr. Ruppersberger is expected to be reelected. This represents a significant change from previous elections in Baltimore County for County Executive where earlier executives were regularly voted out because of voter and employee dissatisfaction with government performance (Platt 1997).

Providing Quality Customer Service

Plans for improving customer service have always been important for business enterprises but only recently have become a strategic goal of public organizations. This change has occurred for several reasons. Large agencies like the USPS face severe competitive pressures from private companies like UPS and Fed Ex and superior customer service is viewed as a competitive advantage.

Governmental entities have traditionally been evaluated by how well the agency adhered to bureaucratic organizing rules. Because of their turbulent operating environments, public operations can no longer organize around bureaucratic norms. Rather, they must now organize around the taxpaying customer's service needs (Sorrell and Lewis 1998).

Public agencies are not use to responding to customer needs. Several basic principles of customer service make this type of responsiveness relatively easy. These include: (1) survey customers to find out what kind and quality of services they want; (2) benchmark performance against "the best in the business;" and (3) the making of information, services, and complaint procedures easily accessible (Roberts 1994).

Local municipalities like Baltimore County, where local schools have already been privatized, are providing better customer service as a response to calls for privatization by taxpayers. Voter demands for better service were the catalyst for both state lawmakers and VDOT officials to implement new pay processes.

The USPS' new way of managing the organization is called CustomerPerfect. The objectives of this organizational process are to obtain new customers, upgrade services to existing customers, and explore new markets. The following, contained in a postal service brochure, explains this focus on customer service:

> CustomerPerfect is a systematic approach to getting the best business results for the Postal Service. It establishes processes to monitor the workplace, create business plans, conduct work, monitor results, initiate improvements, and acknowledge employee contributions (United States Postal Service Publication F-6 1997).

Attracting and retaining customers is a strategic goal of the CustomerPerfect program and USPS managers. Bonus pay is awarded to those managers who reach targeted goals. One market the CustomerPerfect program is focusing on are customers who use private mailbox service provided by firms like PakMail and Mail Boxes Etc.

Obviously, many customers use private boxes as opposed to those offered by the Postal Service. Poor customers service actually created this market in the late 1970s when patrons were told they would have to wait years for post office boxes. This spawned the private box industry.

Private mail box services provide stiff competition for the Customer Service program. For example, private firms offer longer hours and more services than the Postal Service. For USPS managers, bonus pay provides a financial incentive to develop strategies that either compliment or offset these advantages.

The strategic goal of a revised VDOT change strategy, featuring SBP and gainsharing variable pay plans, was the "creation of a highly efficient, customer-oriented culture" (Sorrell and Lewis 1998, 4). This management effort focused on improved customer responsiveness to the agency's improved performance. Customer surveys are distributed in field locations where new pay processes have been implemented.

Strategic goals are then expanded or reformulated based on citizen responses. Flexible, multi-skilled workteams, the result of SBP, allows the agency to shift resources within the organization based on citizen needs. Regularly scheduled community meetings are another way VDOT solicits taxpayer feedback.

New pay plans like gainsharing also allow government to provide specific services that taxpayers desire. The Charlotte, North Carolina gainshare program began in 1994 with the goal of improving services and reducing expenditures. Each department is given a yearly budget reduction target with half of the money saved going back to the city and half being paid out in incentives. By 1997, the city had accumulated savings of $21 million in the general fund and had paid nearly $4 million in gainshare payouts (Risher 1998).

The general fund savings have allowed the police department to add 600 positions. Additional police on the street was a need that citizens had identified. The money saved from gainsharing also allowed the city to forego tax increases for nearly 10 years (Risher 1998).

The "customer" for public organizations are taxpayers who bring pressure on the legislator, through the election process, for improved agency service. Obviously, lawmakers are sensitive to these demands and will often suggest new pay pilot programs to agency heads as a means of meeting voter needs. Clearly, both legislators and public administrators have a vested political interest in expecting that new pay processes trigger appropriate agency responses to customer demands.

Aligning Strategy, Pay, and Performance

As mentioned earlier, strategic transformations require a holistic or integrative approach to organizational change. Organizational systems, values, and philosophy must all be redesigned and aligned to produce the desired strategic goals. New pay concepts are strategic change process that directly trigger this type of "organizational framebending."

Concepts like reinventing government and high-performance government are strategic transformations designed to facilitate alignment of the agency's various subsystems with the strategic goals of the institution. The theoretical basis for systems change is found in Kurt Lewin's behavior-systems framework:

Employees are human beings who are motivated by a vast array of wants and needs. The main focus of organization theory should be on the question of motivation and compliance, and therefore focused on developing theories and prescriptions for motivating employees. ... The focus is on motivating employees and structuring the organization to increase motivation and morale (Dessler 1986, 49).

Although traditional compensation practices have not changed as quickly as other areas of organization design, pay systems are beginning to change in profound ways. New pay concepts are representative of these changes. Research shows that new pay concepts directly influence the organizational issues Lewin discussed -- motivation and organization structure.

New pay schemes often fail to meet their performance objectives because of poor or non-existent alignment between the strategic goals of the change process and the new pay concept(s) utilized. Incongruencies also occur when supportive subsystems are not redesigned to "fit" with the change intervention.

Economists Birecree and Woolley's (1997) analysis of restructuring in Virginia's higher education system provides an excellent example of strategic misalignment. Although one of the goals of restructuring was improved employee relations based on employee involvement, the non-aligned reward system continued to compensate administrators for bureaucratic behaviors. This led to an even greater schism between employees and administrators in Virginia's higher education system on many issues.

Strategic planning is crucial when implementing new pay concepts in public change efforts. Importantly, strategy and pay have to be congruent. Otherwise, the change effort can falter. This was the situation Arlington, Virginia found itself in after implementing SPB in its Public Works Department.

When SBP was introduced in April 1993, a vision statement had been developed. The goal of the effort was relatively straight forward: "To expedite the repair work for Water Main Maintenance by streamlining the production process; promote teamwork, and create a productive, multi-skilled work team" (Department of Public Works - Arlington, VA 1995, 2). Yet, strategic planning, SBP, and the performance management system were not congruent when the new pay system was introduced. The incongruency occurred in two areas -- the failure to developed shared performance measures and the failure to recognize member's acquisition of new skills, both technical and management leadership.

The Arlington SBP plan offers a classic illustration of the dysfunctions created by an incongruency between strategic planning and systems redesign. The poor alignment between strategic pay and redesigned subsystems almost doomed the intervention. Obviously, redesigned assessment and performance evaluation systems were necessary to reward workers under the SBP plan.

Because the non-redesigned appraisal system broke down during the implementation/diffusion phase, the strategy/performance relationship was adversely affected. SBP is a reward-based pay system designed to compensate workers for learning needed organizational skills. Enhanced skills acquisition by employees improves organizational efficiency and performance. However, the motivation to engage in desired institutional behaviors (i.e., skill acquisition and teamwork) was lost in the Arlington intervention simply because there was no appraisal system to assess, and redesigned pay scales to reward, employees for their new behaviors.

The winsharing concept offers a relatively easy way to link strategic goals, new pay rewards, and performance outcomes. Tight budgets and small annual salary increases in the mid-1990s threatened a "brain drain" of professors from Virginia's colleges and universities. Although annual budget increases were incremental, State Council of Higher Education officials believed that spending by departments could be more efficient. Thus, winsharing was introduced. As long as academic and operating standards were met, any money left in a department's annual budget could be spent by department members for any professional reason except salary increases.

This strategic pay process worked well for one fundamental reason -- a clear and direct link between pay and performance has been established by each of these institutions. The winshare administrative record-keeping systems were redesigned to remove structural barriers that would hinder the employees' "clear-line-of-sight" prerequisite for new pay success. Maintaining this "clear-line-of-sight" is crucial to the strategic alignment of strategy, pay, and performance.

For instance, the Georgia Board of Education recently approved $2,000 a year bonuses in 155 schools that developed strategies to help students meet academic goals. This plan requires clearly defined collaborative efforts between teachers, students, administrators, and parents. The clear linkage between pay and performance is established through the Georgia plan.

Using Team-Based Compensation

The public management paradigm links unique public service motivations and congruent reward systems. These types of motivations generally fall into two areas -- norm-based and affective. Research has shown that strategic alignment between new pay processes and public service motivations are best achieved through team-based, as opposed to individual, incentive systems (Perry 1994).

Pay systems influence the creation of organizational culture. In this context, Pfeffer (1998, 118) writes that: "Thinking about teamwork and cooperation and then not having a group-based component to the pay system matters because paying solely on an individual basis signals what the organization believes is actually important -- individual behavior and performance."

The USPS' bonus pay for managers, VDOT's variable pay (workers and managers), Baltimore County's gainshare and SBP plans, and College Station, Texas' (Risher 1998) gainshare plan (the entire city is viewed as a team) all offer examples of team-based compensation systems being successfully implemented in public agencies.

One of the most ambitious team-based bonus performance plans is found in the Roanoke,Virginia Public Schools. Due for full-blown implementation in the 2001-02 school year, the plan offers financial incentives for entire school staffs that meet strategic goals (Shareef 2000b). Teachers will be evaluated in three areas: instruction and student achievement, communications and human relations, and professionalism.

The plan has clearly-defined (and jointly agreed upon) standards and provides greater clarity (than the existing evaluation system) for assessing teacher performance. Both teachers and administrators will be trained in the new evaluation system before it is implemented. Importantly, because of group financial rewards, teachers have an incentive to share, rather than withhold, teaching and classroom management "best practices".

Many teacher unions oppose team-based compensation packages like the Georgia and Roanoke,Virginia plans. They prefer, instead, that performance-based pay be limited to professionally-defined merit, like teacher certification(s). This approach undermines public service motivations outlined by Perry (1994) because of its utilitarian focus on individual merit. The unions' merit-based proposal also bears no clear and direct relationship to the strategic goal -- improved student academic achievement.

Managing the Speed of Systems Change

Because of their political operating environments, public organizations have tended to use much longer time frames in their approach to innovations (Thurow 1996). That is, the innovation is studied, implemented in a pilot program, results are reviewed, and then spread through the organization over an extended period of time. This was the strategy of implementation of SBP in Arlington, Virginia. However, two years into the pilot program, the program coordinator wrote "Because the team's creation involved a big culture change not only within the entire division, a number of social and systematic barriers, or lack of supportive systems, have impeded the envisioned changes" (Department of Public Works - Arlington, VA 1995, 3).

Thus, the Arlington SBP plan had inherent weaknesses before implementation. Strategic planning, devoid of a systems thinking perspective, provided the intervention with little chance of success. What the city planners did learn from the pilot program, however, is that the implementation required a redesigned (1) information system to facilitate two-way flows of information, (2) assessment system to evaluate skill learning and competency, and (3) reward system to compensate for skill(s) acquisition.

While the multiple and simultaneous systems change that many business theorists (Nadler and Tushman 1989) call for create dysfunctions in public organizations, the immediate redesign of relevant supportive subsystems of the new pay plan are required in governmental agencies. At a minimum, this requires the redesign of administrative tasks like record-keeping, performance evaluation systems, and reward structures.

The Roanoke, Virginia team-based compensation plan offers a good example of the "gradualism" and supportive systems realignment that is required in political environments. The school system's administrators initially decided on a bonus-incentive pay plan. A committee of teachers and administrators then took 18 months to develop a means for assessing staff performance. This same committee will then review the city's current teacher plan for "fit" with bonus pay.

In all, it will take approximately 3 1/2 years to implement the new pay plan. Three key supportive subsystems -- information, training and evaluation -- were initially redesigned to be congruent with the bonus pay plan. Other subsystems are considered "lag" variables and will be transformed during diffusion.

The extended timeframe or "gradualism" would not work, because of competitive pressures, in private enterprises using new pay concepts to trigger change. However, because of the political environments that public schools operate in, the Roanoke City Public School's new pay process had to win approval from multiple stakeholders -- the teacher's union, lawmakers, the media (Shareef 2000b) – before introduction. Thus, the 3½ year design, implementation, and diffusion process.

A popular evaluation system, the 360 degree appraisal, can be used when implementing new pay interventions since it "fits" within these processes (Ledford 1998). This evaluation system is grounded in human relations theory, is often implemented during organization change processes, and helps facilitate development of a participative work culture.

The 360-degree performance evaluation would have given Arlington administrators an appraisal process that (1) could assess worker skills achievement and construct appropriate pay rates/scales, (2) provide two way flows of information throughout implementation and diffusion, and (3) created participative subsystems (i.e. information and appraisal) that are congruent with SBP. This appraisal system also is preferred because it better identifies and accurately rewards high and low performers than traditional evaluation systems.

The Utilization of Multiple New Pay Plans

Many theorists are indifferent to whether pay-for-knowledge plans (e.g., SBP) are used in conjunction with pay-for-performance plans (e.g., gainsharing, bonus pay, winsharing, etc.) (Lawler 1992). Yet, the research from public organizations that have jointly used multiple variable pay plans tend to show higher levels of job satisfaction, intrinsic reward satisfactions, and productivity than those who only used a single variable plan.

When VDOT's SBP plan was most effective, employees received base pay, SBP for learning needed skills, and bonus pay for productivity outcomes. The same is true for Baltimore County where workers are compensated through base, gainshare, and SBP plans. The multiple pay plan utilized by College Station, Texas consists of an across-the-board adjustment for all employees, a bonus plan for high performance, and a gainsharing program (Risher 1998).

It appears that the optimal new pay design includes at least two components of variable compensation. Many public organizations using new pay productivity plans already include a defacto pay-for-knowledge system. For instance, while the Georgia state school plan features a $2,000 a year bonus for improving academic performance, it also pays teachers for earning graduate degrees (i.e., pay-for-knowledge).

The USPS also has a tuition-reimbursement plan for employees. So do most police departments. These types of benefits should be explained to workers as part of their total compensation plan. That is, learning needed skills/knowledge leads to greater pay. This multiple and inclusive approach to compensation results in increased worker motivation and performance.

One component of new pay -- indirect benefits -- is hardly used in public organizations. This is a serious mistake. It would be relatively easy to link and reward desired strategic outcomes (e.g., better attendance, improved productivity, etc.) with changed behaviors (e.g., weight loss, smoking cessation, and stress management) that directly influence desired organizational goals. The under-utilization of indirect benefits in new pay interventions occurs because Human Resource Management (HRM) departments are usually excluded from strategic decision-making and planning in public agencies.

The transforming power of new pay processes are not fully realized when indirect benefits are excluded from the strategic pay intervention. In order for HRM to become a strategic partner, it must develop value-driven "organizational capabilities" that directly link indirect benefits to the strategic objectives of the change process. As Lawler (1995, 9) wrote, "The challenge for the human resource function is to identify what better performance means and then become expert in the kind of organizational policies and practices that produce it."

Implications

Senior managers function as both leaders and managers in public sector pay processes. They provide direction, solicit feedback, and share results about organizational performance. It is also important that the executive leadership team "model" behaviors (Bennis 1989) they expect to be demonstrated throughout the organization. Consequently, leadership behavior becomes another alignment issue -- executive leaders/managers modeling behaviors that are congruent with the strategic goal of the new pay intervention.

The top public executive, however, is the trigger for new pay processes in governmental agencies. Postmaster General Runyon initially presented the idea of a short-term incentive system to enhance performance to the Postal Service Governors. Baltimore County

Executive Dutch Ruppersberger was the driving force behind the implementation of gainsharing and SBP. Skill-based pay in the VDOT and winsharing in Virginia's colleges and universities were highly touted policies of former Governor George Allen.

Economist Lester Thurow (1980) often talks about how short-term political horizons create win/lose situations for public organizations. As he notes, politicians need "to deliver" at election time. This means public administrators have to utilize time-based performance outcomes that coincide with the election/political cycle when implementing new pay plans. The political cycle described by Thurow allows public change agents to gear strategic management processes, especially performance assessment and budgetary requests, with relevant election periods. Successful pilot programs help insure continued political support for the new pay effort.

Improving customer service represents a new area of activity for most public agencies. Traditionally operating in monopolistic environments, governmental entities have not responded well to taxpayer demands for better service. Privatization, downsizing, and outsourcing have all combined to make improved customer service a priority for all public agencies -- even the IRS.

To improve customer service, public employees need a broad understanding of how the organization works. That is, public sector workers need business education. Keeping employees informed of the constant challenges the agency faces creates a "shared reality" that both the employee and worker must accept if the enterprise is to remain viable.

Better customer service processes are relatively easy to implement since they involve basic human relations skills. For instance, the handling of customer inquiries and delivery of services with courtesy is both a customer service dynamic and human relations skill. The same customer service/human relations mix is evident when the public agency provides pleasant surrounding for customers seeking redress for poor services.

As an indication of its priority, both the USPS and VDOT have made excellent customer service the strategic objective of their new pay-driven change process.

Team-based compensation plans are congruent with traditional public service motivations. Individual incentive plans are not. New pay plans encourage teamwork and the sharing of "best practices" between both intra and inter organizational units. The design of the Roanoke City Public School's teacher pay-for-performance plan offers an excellent model for agencies interested in linking new pay strategies and public service motivations.

The Roanoke School System's new pay plan also provides an excellent example of "gradualism" and the use of parallel structures for organizations facilitating change in political environments. The 3½ year planning and design process would be prohibitive in business organizations. Ledford (1998, 16) cautions against both the pilot program and gradual approach in the design of new pay systems:

> Changes in business conditions mean that any specific pay experiment will be of limited relevance elsewhere before the diffusion takes hold. ... The careful and slow approach often mobilizes opposition to the innovation because it remains different and threatening to the bulk of the organization that is using older, more familiar practices.

Ironically, just the opposite occurs with institutions operating in political environments -- perceived quickness of change mobilizes opposition from major stakeholders like unions, politicians, and the media. Gaining support from these powerful interests is simply a slow and gradual process. However, endorsement of the new pay venture from these stakeholders -- especially media elites -- is considered a political coup for public sector change agents. Pilot programs provide political payoffs during the initial stages of implementation. Public administration leaders would do well to link performance evaluations of new pay processes with political reelection cycles.

New pay practices in public organizations are driven by political and public service motivational, not market, dynamics. As such, new pay must be adapted to meet these unique determinants. The High Performance Government model provides an excellent framework for these practices to be operationalized.

Redesign issues are essential components in new pay implementations. Some pay plans like winsharing only require minimum redesign procedures and are essentially self-managing. Others, like SBP and bonus pay, require a quick redesign of both the administrative record-keeping and performance evaluation systems. Several redesign determinants for new pay success in public organizations have emerged. It appears that the information, appraisal, reward, and training systems have to be realigned during the initial stages of implementation. Other subsystems can be aligned later during diffusion.

More complicated pay systems like the USPS' EVA based bonus plan not only require systems redesign but extensive business education for employees. Workers have to possess an economic understanding of how they add "value" to the agency's business operations. Complex systems like EVA demand on-going training so workers don't lose "clear vision" between pay and performance.

The utilization of multiple new pay systems appear to be more successful in achieving improved performance than reliance on a single new pay approach. Concepts like winsharing should be presented as part of an overall compensation plan and linked directly with desired efficiency standards. This type of linkage helps improve both (1) intrinsic/influence/job satisfactions and (2) agency performance.

Indirect benefits are hardly used in new pay interventions because of poor HRM alignment with agency strategic objectives. Recent research (Rainey 1994; Barringer and Milkovich 1998) shows that the major objective of HRM departments who implement flexible benefit plans was to control costs. Little attention is paid by HRM departments to the issue of performance.

"Organizational capabilities" reflect both the strategic goals of the agency and HRM alignment with the over-arching strategy. The issue of indirect benefits provides a good opportunity for these departments to become involved in new pay processes. Much of the initiative for this involvement must come from HRM Directors.

Successful variable pay plans provide political payoffs for elected officials through improved efficiency, cost savings, and enhanced customer service. Moreover, new pay plans are "alien" to public organizations only when they are incongruent with the agencies political operating environment, value-orientation, and work motivations. As public stewards, the leader and executive team have to design new pay plans for "fit" with these three environmental determinants. This list of "best practices" provide a platform for creating that congruency.

Chapter 3

Seven Common Errors of Public Organizations Implementing New Pay Processes

A change model that has been designed for implementing new pay processes in political entities has been presented.   In addition, successful implementation processes by numerous public agencies have been outlined. So, it would be easy to assume that all a public sector leader would have to do is take this change blueprint, operationalize the concepts, and trigger successful agency transformations.

Unfortunately, strategic organization change in public (as well as private) organizations is never so easy.   A major reason for the difficulty is the political nature of organizations.   For private sector firms, politics are primarily internal.   For public agencies, an analysis of organizational politics -- relations between interests, conflict, and power -- focuses both on internal and external dynamics.

Morgan (1986) notes that a negative view of politics keeps us from recognizing that politics and politicking are an essential part of organizational life -- not something optional, extra, or dysfunctional. He also reminds us that the original meaning of the word "politics" provided a framework for society's divergent interests to reconcile their differences through consultation and negotiation.   What ultimately decides how these issues are resolved is the political culture of the organization -- autocratically (we'll do it this way); bureaucratically (we're suppose it do it this way); technocratically (it's best to do it this way); or democratically (how shall we do it?).

Most public organizations continue to be administered either autocratically or bureaucratically (Shareef 1994b). Consequently, they fall back into "cognitive cultural traps" when implementing new pay processes that inherently create high-involvement or democratic decision-making cultures. The anti-democratic nature of public organizations not only (1) reduces the value of the workplace experience for workers and (2) undermines public trust by the lack of citizen involvement, it also causes political actors to engage in predictable patterns of behaviors that frustrate organizational change processes.

Seven predictable traps of public organization change are:

- The failure to create high-involvement work cultures.

- The failure to improve labor-management relations.

- The failure to include public administration scholars/managers in the design of new pay processes.

- The failure to use "policy entrepreneurs" during the change process.

- The failure to have enough funds "at risk" to motivate.

- The failure to understand that merit pay is not a new pay process.

- The failure to distinguish between incremental and strategic pay.

The Failure to Create
High-Involvement Work Cultures

Slater and Bennis (1990, 167) wrote that democracy is inevitable "because it is the only system that can successfully cope with the changing demands of contemporary civilization in business as well as government." These writers saw democratization of the workplace as encompassing a system of values that included free and full communication (regardless of rank and power), a reliance on consensus rather than on coercion, and an atmosphere that encourages expression. Industrial democracy/employee involvement plans play a significant role in new pay strategies since workers have input in aligning design features to fit with the strategic vision. Through this process, workers become value-added resources contributing to the effectiveness of the change process.

However, most public organizations (even those implementing new pay processes) retain bureaucratic, top-down cultures. Research has shown that managers are the organizational stakeholders that most resist these shifts in decision-making and power (Klein 1984). A perfect example of managerial resistance to change occurred when VDOT administrators decided to unilaterally, even in the midst of an evolving participative culture, force everyone into the SBP plan.

This move was made after many VDOT managers reported feelings of "losing control" as a result of the SBP process (Shareef 1998). The agency's workers, as political constituents, reacted to the elimination of the dual compensation system by contacting state lawmakers. While this gained VDOT workers some political leverage and power against management, it devalued the new pay process in the eyes of many lawmakers and the public.

This same type of struggle has manifested in the USPS over variable bonus pay. The plan was implemented through pilot programs for managers with diffusion for workers to come later.

However, workers (especially letter carriers) see Postal Service productivity coming primarily from their improved efficiency but only management being rewarded for the enhanced performance (Shareef 1999b). In effect, these workers are expressing (in)equity concerns over the bonus pay plan.

The USPS has a terrible history of including employees in meaningful decision-making and remains a rigid, bureaucratic culture (Shareef 1999b). Postal workers do not believe they will ever see the monetary benefits of their enhanced efficiency because of the top-down power equation. Like their VDOT counterparts, and because they are excluded from decision-making processes, they have begun to see sinister motives behind the new pay intervention (Shareef 1999a).

Studies show that variable pay innovations will only succeed in high-involvement cultures (Lawler 1998; Ledford 1998). Public sector leaders only undermine employee and public trust, and gain short-term benefits, when they utilize new pay processes in autocratic/bureaucratic work cultures. However, from both a short and long-term perspective, the struggle by managers to maintain organizational control merely hinders organizational performance thereby accelerating calls for privatization or outsourcing.

Despite its linkage with participative cultures, variable pay plans are often used to straighten existing bureaucratic values. Short-term gains are a hallmark of bureaucratic cultures. When the State of Virginia restructured its higher education system, and announced it desired more input from faculty, the reward system only compensated administrators for short-term cost reductions. This resulted in the ... "system being restructured away from a relatively more cooperative one to one that increasingly exhibits features of a destructive system" (Birecree and Woolley 1997, 114).

On the other hand, the Roanoke, Virginia School System's bonus pay plan involved 35 teachers in the 52-person strategic planning committee. Administrators wanted to avoid developing a performance appraisal system that tied teacher pay with outcomes that were not within their control. Consequently, because of teacher involvement in the design alignment of the performance evaluation system, the change effort has been endorsed by both the teachers and their union.

The nature of work in contemporary public organizations is now more technological, scientific, and interactive. Public sector work is also generally more labor-intensive than in business enterprises. This type of work demands open or democratic cultures since bureaucratic forms of organizing restrict the flow of information in the modern workplace.

Those who do the work know better than anyone else does what skills, knowledge, and resources are needed to improve organizational performance. As we shall see later, worker input is essential in the design of new pay processes since only they know how much money is needed to motivate. Public leaders have to understand that new pay processes are the catalyst for high-involvement work cultures.

These work cultures provide a framework for resolving issues of power and resource allocation. Bureaucratic cultures don't. New pay processes have to also be designed to reward managers for high-involvement, but not bureaucratic, behaviors.

The Failure to Improve
Labor-Management Relations

The Winter Commission report (1993, 46) suggested that improved labor-management relations were crucial in creating high-performance government. Specifically, the report stated:

> ... Management, for its part, must start including workers, including union leadership, in decision-making processes from the start, and not simply brief staff "from on high" at the end. Early engagement of staff is a hallmark of the current quest for quality management, a factor too often ignored by those government executives who remain mired in a command and control mentality.

Adversial labor-management relations can prove fatal to otherwise effective new pay interventions. Again, the USPS bonus plan is illustrative. On June 10, 1999, members of the National Association of Letter Carriers held nationwide "informational pickets" to inform the public about heavier workloads without corresponding pay increases. In particular, they feel that the bonuses that postal managers get, and they do not, are a result of their increased performance (Kane 1999).

The Postal Services' union should have had significant input in the design and implementation of the bonus pay plan. Given the history of mistrust between labor and management in the agency, their input was especially needed during the design and diffusion process. As the Winter Commission report concluded, union collaboration can be an important ally in creation of high-performance work systems.

On the other hand, Baltimore County, Maryland included union officials in every phase of the gainsharing intervention. This was true even though union leaders initially opposed the new pay plan. These leaders were especially prominent on the Internal Review Committee -- the group that approves or disapproves each front-line proposal that goes to the County Executive.

James Clark, President of the Baltimore County Federation of Public Employees, wrote the following concerning gainsharing:

> Another positive in 1997 was the expansion of the gainsharing process. As many of you know, we were originally against the program when the original pilot programs were launched. Having had an opportunity to be part of this year's review committee, I now have a different view. The proposals submitted by the employees involved demonstrated what we have said all along. The people in the field know their job best. They know what works and what doesn't, and they know how to work efficiently. The boost in morale was evident in every single participant (Office of Personnel - Baltimore County 1998, 3).

Unions are political entities who are interested in money, job security, and control over the work environment. Research shows that unions rarely adversely affect productivity outcomes. The general conclusion now is that "it is the state of labor relations rather than unions and collective bargaining per se that determines productivity" (Pfeffer 1998, 228).

Consequently, poor labor-management relations will likely affect productivity gains made through the USPS' CustomerPerfect/bonus plan. Conversely, because of good labor-management relations in Baltimore County, both improved employee morale and productivity increases can be expected to continue. Continuing the traditional adversal labor-management relations in a highly competitive and demanding environment is foolhardy.

Because "information strikes" like those conducted by the carrier's union appeal to the public, they have both business and political ramifications. Since letter carriers have personal contact with the public, patrons may decide to use services by competitors in support of the union cause. Or, the public may strongly voice their objections to rate increases (through the media or legislative process) if profits are seen as only benefiting management (Shareef 1999b).

In this political process, unions should be equal partners with management in the design and diffusion of the new pay intervention. Maintaining the adversial labor-management system ultimately results in the loss of public respect and support. At a time when agencies are attempting to restore public accountability, exclusion of unions from the management process is inexcusable.

The Failure to Include Public Administration Scholars and Managers in the Design of New Pay Processes

Public administration scholars and managers, those who value ideas like civic duty and public trust, are often excluded from the design of new pay processes in their formative stages. More often than not, it is business professors who shape the process at this critical juncture. Because of a focus on bottom-line results, and ignoring public administration values/motivations, these processes start off with little chance of success.

The VDOT variable pay process was initially designed by two professors from the University of Virginia's Darden School of Business. The use of UVA business professors as consultants on this project is especially illustrative since the highly regarded Cooper Center for Public Service, which specializes in public sector change, is also located on the UVA campus. This type of selection is not uncommon when it comes to public sector change processes.

The USPS' bonus pay system -- based on a complicated economic formula known as Economic Value Added (EVA) -- was developed by a Wall Street Investment firm. This financial performance management system was used previously by Wal-Mart, IBM, Coca-Cola, and CSX before being adopted by the USPS. Many of the political problems encountered by EVA, and worker reactions to those problems, could not have been anticipated by Wall Street investors.

Even successful new pay processes like Baltimore County's gainsharing/SBP were designed by private sector consultants. The primary consultant for VDOT is now PricewaterhouseCoopers. I recently asked one of the consultants if he considered how legislators perceived the change process at VDOT? He replied that "I don't know -- I'm only interested in the business side of change".

Politicians also overlook the expertise that public administration managers and professors bring to the change process. After being elected Governor of Virginia in 1994, Governor George Allen initiated a strike force to reform state government. Most of its 60 members were drawn from the private sector.

Roberts (1994, 7) wrote the following concerning the composition of the Governor's strike force:

> While bringing in respected and talented people from the private sector, the governor should give them partners in government with whom to work, inviting state employees to be their 'best professional selves' and make significant contributions to redeploying services for better quality and results. State employees live daily with bureaucratic nonsense and inefficiency. ... Their input should be listened to thoughtfully.

Furthermore, Roberts notes that the real work of implementation will come from reenergized employees who become advocates because of feelings of ownership. New pay processes are not aided by an uninspired, passive, or alienated public workforce. These processes also are not aided when the theoretical and field-based knowledge of public administration scholars is not solicited.

These points should be remembered by chief executives when developing strategic planning teams or hiring consultants to design new pay processes for public organizations.

As mentioned earlier, this exclusion from the strategic planning process partially results from the poor relations that public administration scholars and managers have with media writers who report on management and organizational performance. These writers generally view the field of public administration as deterministic (i.e., bureaucratic). Moreover, many business professors or MBAs are seen as antideterministic or believing that innovative management practices can improve productivity outcomes.

Most media business writers also possess an antideterminist ideology (Chen and Meindl 1991). They tend to construct more favorable images of leaders and managers who are antideterministic.

Consequently, when the problems of agency performance become a public issue, these writers promote scholars who they believe can positively impact the problem.

Since the media -- along with interest groups and politicians -- constitute the public organization's operating environment, it seems strange that those who shape images for public consumption are alienated from those who best understand public organizations. If public administration scholars are going to be involved in shaping policy concerning new pay transformations, they must convey to media writers an antideterministic belief about the organizational change process. Otherwise, the media will continue to promote (1) business professors as change agents and (2) private sector leaders to head public organizations even though their (i.e., business professors and private sector leaders) transformative strategies repeatedly fail.

Ironically, many public administration scholars are also antideterministic. Our "work product" is usually found in scholarly journals. Our work should also be increasingly seen on the editorial pages of the nation's newspapers and in popular media publications discussing pay innovations in public agencies.

I've done quite a bit of this type of "editorial writing" and have been surprised at the number of calls from media representatives seeking information on broad public policy and organization change issues (Shareef 1994c). My editorial positions, clearly antideterministic, also resulted in me writing a weekly online public management/policy column for a large newspaper chain. Furthermore, the newspaper column has generated inquiries from other media outlets requesting comments concerning specific change activities in public organizations.

A dominant cultural value of the American press is an antideterministic view of organizational life. These values should be remembered by public administration theorists and managers. Bringing congruency or "fit" between media values and public administration norms remains a challenge for both groups.

The Failure to Use "Policy Entrepreneurs" During the Change Process

Public organizations need full-time and fully qualified policy entrepreneurs who act as a buffer between the agency's new pay intervention and various institutional stakeholders including legislators, interest groups, taxpayers, and the media. These policy entrepreneurs serve as an "information clearinghouse" concerning fundamental issues

-- rationale for the change, strategic goals, timetables, etc. -- concerning the transformation.

Lawmakers especially need a knowledgeable resource that provides a continuous flow of information and updates about the change endeavor. Given the 2, 4, and 6 year election cycle, this type of information is crucial for legislators handling inquires from the media or interest groups and crafting policy positions. The policy entrepreneur becomes an indispensable link between the change intervention and political actors who fund and support the process.

This type of relationship is needed with the media as well. Public organizations involved in new pay processes clearly show an anti-deterministic bent. Thus, they are very likely to receive favorable coverage -- and image construction -- from media outlets. Policy entrepreneurs are needed to cultivate that type of image construction with those who shape images for the public.

The organization's culture will determine what role policy entrepreneurs play in the new pay process. Bureaucratic cultures will resist creating two-way flows of information about the intervention. Participative or organic institutions will do just the opposite.

Information in both the USPS and VDOT about their new pay interventions are shrouded in secrecy, covered under layers of bureaucracy. There is no one office or person where information is forthcoming about the intervention. Other public agencies who are interested in design, implementation, and diffusion issues find it difficult to get answers about the new pay intervention.

Baltimore County, on the other hand, offers a good agency model for handling public relations about their pay interventions. All inquiries about gainsharing or SBP are routed through the Office of Personnel. Director of Personnel Antony Sharbaugh or Program Coordinator Melissa Boone are personable, articulate, and highly professional in their handling of inquiries about these programs. They are "designated" information resources for the change intervention.

The result? Variable pay interventions in Baltimore County receive much more favorable media coverage that similar processes in the USPS and VDOT. Coverage of the Baltimore County intervention ranges from the local media to professional journals/magazines to national publications like the Wall Street Journal.

Many of these outlets acknowledge Melissa Boone as their contact person. She is accessible to lawmakers and interested parties as well. It is worth noting that the Baltimore County program continues to receive high approval ratings from workers, politicians, and taxpayers.

Recently, I conducted a leadership workshop with administrators of a small town. Afterwards, the Police Chief asked me about implementing a gainsharing program. I made several suggestions and directed him to Melissa Boone of Baltimore County. He recently contacted me and stated that his discussions with this "policy entrepreneur" were invaluable in his conceptualization of the gainsharing pay plan.

The same situation exists in Charlotte, North Carolina where Ken Wallace, the City's Compensation and Benefits Manager, handles most inquiries about the gainshare program. Like Baltimore County, all inquiries are routed through his office. This type of public relations structure is similar to those established in highly successful private companies like Southwest Airlines.

Public organizations operate in volatile political environments where media and interest groups can create turbulence because of the lack of information. Policy entrepreneurs "smooth" out the often turbulent relationship between agencies undergoing change and important stakeholders. Policy entrepreneurship, like new pay processes, clearly "fits" in a participative work culture but not in bureaucracies.

The Failure of Not Having Enough
Funds "at Risk" to Motivate

New pay interventions are permanent changes in notions about compensation, motivation, and performance. They are not simply passing management fads. Public leaders, before designing and implementing new pay processes, have to be relatively sure that enough funds are available to actually motivate workers. Two important issues have to be resolved in public agencies before new pay processes can be implemented: (1) employees have to provide meaningful input, in addition to wage surveys, on how much money will motivate (i.e., this cannot be a top-down decision); and (2) there has to be a commitment from legislators to fund the new pay intervention, at least through the pilot stages.

In a participative culture, satisfying the first issue should be easy. Meeting the second requirement is more difficult. The financing of monetary rewards for public employees simply have to be included as incentives in the budget. Otherwise, failure to provide rewards based on employee expectations can severely threaten new pay programs.

Another problem that can negatively affect the new pay-employee motivation relationship is when workers "top out". This occurs when employees reach a structural barrier and are either no longer eligible for further pay increases or receive only incremental pay adjustments. These structural impediments occur when existing classifications have not been redesigned for congruency with new pay interventions.

The case of Michael Riley, USPS Budget Director, is a case-in-point. Postal managers are eligible for bonuses of up to $12,000 each based on the agency's performance and customer satisfaction. Since federal salaries are capped at $148,000, many higher-paid directors do not get their full bonus. In 1997, Riley was eligible for $47,000 bonus but the salary cap trimmed that to $400 - or $260 after taxes (The Roanoke Times 1997).

Pay classification systems redesign, along with committed political support and employee input, provide a framework that allows variable pay plans to deliver on their promise -- providing monetary incentives that lead to higher performance.

The Failure to Understand that
Merit Pay is Not a New Pay Process

The merit pay concept is so widely accepted that most American organizations consider themselves employing a merit system. These pay systems are designed to give pay increases to individuals based on their superior's evaluation of performance. Merit pay plans are thought to both enhance motivation and retain better performers by establishing a clear link between rewards and performance.

However, there is considerable evidence that merit pay does not create this direct link between pay and performance. There are several reasons for this breakdown (Lawler 1987, 21-24):

- Poor Performance Measures - Good measures of organization or group performance exist, but similar measure are not available for individuals. In the absence of good objective measures of individuals performance, most rely on the judgements of managers. These judgements are often seen by subordinates as invalid, unfair, and discriminatory.

- Poor Communication - Because of poor communications about pay and performance, employees are asked to believe (as an article of faith), that pay and performance are related. In most organizations, all employees get pay increases because of inflation and labor market changes. This often causes individuals to question how much "merit" had to do with their merit increases.

- Poor Delivery System - The typical merit salary increase is particularly poor at actually relating pay to performance because it allows for only small changes in total pay to occur in one year. Often, only a few percentage points separate the raises given to good performance and those given to poor performances.

- Poor Managerial Behaviors - Managers do a number of things that adversely affect the perceived and actual connection between pay and performance. Perhaps most serious is the failure to recommend widely different pay increases for subordinates when large differences in performance exist. ... One reason for this seems to be the unpleasant task of explaining why someone got a low raise.

In addition to poor linkages between pay and performance, merit pay systems are inherently a zero-sum game. Since the manager is operating with a "pay raise budget" that's a percentage of the units' total salary budget, the more one worker gets, the less is left for colleagues. Consequently, merit pay creates rivalries between individual within units.

Merit pay systems also increase antagonisms between intraorganizational units by creating a financial disincentive for employees to share "best operating practices" and learning from workers in other parts of the organization. The Roanoke, Virginia Public Schools dropped a merit pay plan in favor of a bonus pay because of this issue (Shareef 2000b). Pfeffer (1998) concludes that the dysfunctions of merit pay affects motivation, productivity, and organizational learning.

Public organizations have not had good experiences with merit pay. Several theorists have discussed the linkage problems between pay and performance (Pfeffer 1998; Agim 1994; Perry 1990). The research by Pearce, Stevenson, and Perry (1985) in the Social Security Administration found no differences in performance after merit pay was introduced as part of civil service reform. The results of this study are especially compelling since merit pay raises were contingent on clear performance objectives in an attempt to alleviate the linkage problem.

Merit pay is not a "new pay" concept but is often promoted as part of a variable pay plan. This is a grave error. As discussed in this section, it is difficult to link merit pay to productivity outcomes, the concept fosters individual rather than team performance, and the percentage of pay increase between high and low performers is often not enough to motivate. All of these factors, and a lack of "at risk" funds, undermined a merit pay-for-performance plan designed to reward members of high-performing teams in Oregon (Oregon Department of Transportation 1995).

The Failure to Distinguish Between Strategic and Incremental Change

Often, strategic planners do not distinguish between the two types of organizational change -- strategic and incremental. Strategic change impacts the entire organization and fundamentally redefines what the organization is and changes its basic framework. These changes include transformations in strategy, structure, people, process, and core values (Nadler and Tushman 1980). Roberts' HPG model/new pay processes represent strategic change interventions.

Conversely, incremental changes are designed to enhance the effectiveness of the organization but within the existing strategy, mode of organizing, and value orientation. The utility worker concept, utilizing cross training to enhance employee flexibility, represents an incremental change process.

This distinction is crucial since using an incremental approach to facilitate new pay change invariably results in a failed change effort. The City of Arlington, Virginia, for example, created a wonderful mission statement for its SBP change intervention but never created the proper alignment between strategy and a redesigned administrative and appraisal system for the intervention to succeed. Neither was there alignment between the strategic goals of the intervention and creation of a participative culture and supportive open information systems.

Arlington administrators and consultants proceeded as if the systems needed to compliment or support SBP would automatically align themselves with the new pay intervention. Perhaps, they thought these systems could be aligned at a later, more convenient date. In all likelihood, they did not recognize the reinforcing nature of organizational systems (Shareef 1993).

This lack of recognition reflects the incremental thinking-mindset found in most organizations considering new pay concepts. Clearly, this type of world-view represents poor conceptual understanding of strategic change processes. The failure to distinguish between incremental and strategic change has been cited as a causal factor for the poor change outcomes in several public agencies (Shareef 1998, 1994b).

Variable pay interventions trigger strategic changes throughout the entire organization. These changes do not occur within the existing organizing culture or value orientation. Public sector leaders should carefully consider the total agency impact of variable pay processes when considering their utilization.

Implications

New pay plans inherently trigger high-involvement or participative work cultures. Many of the management sins committed during the implementation and diffusion of these pay processes attempt to stifle workplace democracy. These management practices also hinder community involvement in decision-making processes.

Managers attempt to undermine the creation of participative cultures for several reasons. Many fear the loss of power and status when workers are empowered. Some are legitimately concerned that empowered workers, and self-managing teams, will cause them to be downsized out of their jobs.

Strategic change visions often neglect the concerns of the managerial group. This is a costly mistake. Agency leaders must address the employment security concerns of managers if they truly desire new pay success. One way to address these concerns is to outline the role/function of managers in a redesigned agency during the strategic visioning process. Another is to use the managerial group as the lead "change lever" in transformation or introduce competency-based pay for managers early in the change intervention (Chapter 5).

Public organizations operate in extremely turbulent and demanding environments. Unlike their private sector counterparts, they are accountable to numerous stakeholders. Consequently, information about new pay change processes should be readily available and accessible to politicians, the media, and taxpayers. Agencies who handle this task well are perceived to be well-managed and innovative. This enhances the prospects for continued financing for variable pay plans and inclusion of public managers and scholars in the initial stages of new pay design.

The common errors of not (1) creating participative cultures, (2) improving labor-management relations, and (3) utilizing policy entrepreneurs committed by public leaders are a direct result of bureaucratic cultures. As Kanter (1983) noted, segmentalist organizations stifle innovation. Until there is a commitment by agency leaders to facilitate a shift from bureaucratic to high-involvement work cultures, new pay plans have no chance of succeeding in public organizations.

Yet, it is impossible to make this cultural shift without agency planners and consultants conceptually understanding the difference between incremental and strategic transformations. This is an acute area of the new pay change process where the knowledge of antideterministic public administration scholars would be invaluable. Public sector change agents consistently fail to appreciate this distinction. Thus, when their change efforts fail, these leaders are viewed as inept or incompetent, especially by the media.

Moreover, there are huge political costs for not making the strategic/incremental distinction. Political leaders, under pressure from the public and media, want successful change processes. The expedient solution when this doesn't occur -- lure a private sector executive to run the contemporary public organization.

Consequently, because of specific value - orientations of the business press (Chen and Meindl 1991) (which will be further discussed in Chapter 6), the "private-is-better" approach becomes legitimated in the minds of the agency's stakeholders. This results in public administration theorists and managers being excluded from the planning and decision-making loop concerning new pay interventions. This cycle is so common partly because of the bureaucratic image that media writers have about public administration theorists and practitioners.

Chapter 4

Strategic Change: Starting at the
Top or Bottom

Strategic change processes present leaders, managers, and consultants with an interesting implementation question: Which group -- employees or managers -- should be the initial target group of the new pay plan. Early organizational cultural transformations focused on workers and viewed managers as a "lag variable" that could be changed later.

However, a mounting body of research (Walton and Schlesinger 1979; Shareef 1989, 1998) found that managers sabotaged these change processes because of perceived threats to (1) institutional power and (2) job security.

As a result of this management resistance, researchers at the University of Southern California's Center for Effective Organizations reported impressive change outcomes when managers become the target group in the transformative process. Mohrman and Lawler (1988, 19) explain:

> We have suggested organizations transitioning to high involvement cultures might benefit by making managerial behavior a lead change lever rather than a lag change variable. In our experience, it is the variable most likely to undermine all other changes and cause the organization to revert back to traditional practices.

Most public organizations have focused on targeting workers for the new pay plan with managerial changes coming later. However, it appears that the size (Child 1973) of the agency may be the determinant that best dictates which target group should be the lead change lever. Smaller municipalities like Baltimore County, College Station, Texas and the Roanoke City Public Schools have had success targeting workers as the primary change variable. Conversely, larger agencies like the USPS and VDOT have experienced managerial resistance over strategic change processes that began with workers.

A brief example should help clarify size/decentralization issues for organizations operating in political environments. I have previously discussed the design of a bonus pay plan in the Roanoke City Schools. Initiated by the Superintendent, the new pay concept and redesign plan were approved by the school board, the system's executive committee, and union in fairly rapid succession. Regardless, it will take a total of 3½ years to implement this pay plan in a mid-sized school district.

Conversely, consider the current proposal of Virginia Governor James Gilmore for the state's colleges to sign performance contracts in exchange for their public financing (Hebel 2000). The contract period is for six years wherein the colleges would predict their budgets and agree, in return for long-term financing, to meet performance goals. No other state in the country directly links public financing with institutional performance in this manner.

There are 15 public colleges in Virginia and a large community college system. Each university, and the two-year college system, would negotiate separately with the state based on the institution's mission. Because of the size of higher education in the state, and the myriad of institutional missions, it has taken 18 months to simply reach tentative agreement on the various performance goals for each institution.

Another group of stakeholders -- members of the General Assembly -- have traditionally controlled state funds for higher education. The Governor's plan would remove these legislators from the funding process. Reluctant to relinquish their power, members of the General Assembly have created their own committee to assess how the state's colleges should be funded. Protecting their political turf, the state's lawmakers have not bought into the idea of decentralized decisionmaking by college presidents.

In reality, neither has Governor Gilmore who has attempted to micromanage the whole process. This despite the fact that the Winter Commission has warned that executive micromanaging undermines decentralization and creates integrity problems for the change process. However, the Governor has higher political aspirations and wants the performance-funding plan to be the centerpiece of his administrative legacy. He would like to see the plan implemented by 2002, the last year of his term.

This is unlikely to occur. Because of both the Governor's and legislative interference, college president's have not felt fully empowered in this process. Many are trying to wait until the Governor leaves office before signing an agreement. Most like the plan but the size of the higher education system in the state, coupled with executive and administrative meddling, have left the college presidents feeling like bystanders. They almost uniformly believe the plan cannot be implemented by 2002.

Roanoke City School Superintendent E. Wayne Harris has fewer stakeholders, personnel, and operating units than the state's higher education system. He also has no political ambitions. Still, it will take him 3½ years to decentralize decisionmaking and implement a bonus pay plan for teachers. Governor Gilmore's task is much more complex because of the size of Virginia's higher education system and he will probably be out of office before decentralization takes place.

Obviously, size is a major determinant of how quickly decentralization can be diffused through an organization. This axiom, coupled with multiple stakeholders that shape the public agency's political environment, makes new pay implementation in the enterprises slow when compared to what occurs in business firms. Even small public institutions need a longer time-horizon (e.g., 4-5 years) to successfully introduce a new pay intervention than a comparably-sized private organization.

Managerial Behavior, Strategic Change, and the USPS

The USPS has a long history of managerial resistance to strategic transformations. Consequently, the agency implemented its bonus pay plan, as Morhman and Lawler suggested, with the managerial group. Since implementation four years ago, productivity and effectiveness have increased dramatically. For the first time since the agency became quasi-private, it has made a profit for several consecutive years.

The USPS strategy was to initially implement bonus pay in the managerial group and then diffuse the pay system throughout the organization. After all, it is the union members (letter carriers, clerks, maintenance workers, etc.) who do the actual "heavy lifting" that produce increased organizational efficiencies. However, the diffusion of bonus pay has yet to occur in the agency.

Consequently, worker morale has suffered. In June 1999, letter carriers held "informational pickets" in front of post offices nationwide demanding fair compensation for their efforts in helping the agency achieve high levels of productivity (Shareef 1999a). Not being included in the bonus plan has increased already strained union-management relations in the organization.

The failure to push bonus pay benefits to the rank and file has created legitimate (in)equity issues for workers in the agency. The informational pickets are one way to reduce these feelings of inequity. USPS leadership has offered no reasonable explanations to the unions why these economic benefits are not being shared.

The agency's impressive productivity gains are threatened by employee inequity feelings. Typically workers mitigate feelings of inequity by reducing inputs or outcomes when and where it is advantageous (Adams 1977). These reductions usually negatively impact performance results since workers will decrease their efforts (for reasons of psychological well-being) to a level that does not produce punitive organizational sanctions.

Changing Managerial Behavior with Strategic Pay

Strategy and pay reflect an organization's values and also drives performance. Thus, strategic pay should be directly linked with managerial behaviors in new pay interventions. In the USPS example, strategic pay for managers should not only be tied to efficient quantitative outcomes but also to how quickly bonus pay is diffused throughout the organization. Agency-wide diffusion was not a strategic goal of the USPS bonus pay plan; thus, managers had very little motivation to diffuse the pay plan.

By rewarding managers for behaviors that did not speed diffusion of bonus pay to union members, the agency's leadership sent a message to the managerial group that diffusion through the ranks was not important. This omission threatens the long-term effectiveness of the agency. Effective performance practices help organizational performers know what they are supposed to do, provide feedback, and reward activities that link these performers to the mission of the organization:

> The performance management practices shape performances by giving information about appropriate content and direction of activities. Ideally, they also align the performances of the various performers in the organization so that their organizational activities aggregate to deliver effective and efficient performance to the overall organizational mission (Morhman and Morhman 1997, 5-6).

Agencies that implement new pay plans that target management should articulate two strategic objectives: a direct link between managerial compensation and institutionalization of the pay plan to avoid equity concerns/performance declines and the institutionalization of new pay should occur within two years of implementation in the management ranks.

VDOT and Skill-Based Pay Implementation

This agency utilized the traditional implementation strategy of targeting union members for the new pay intervention. The agency anticipated managerial resistance when it developed its strategic plan for implementing SBP and included competency-based pay for managers. However, the strategic plan did not have specific timetables for implementing managerial competency pay.

After two years of successfully diffusing SBP to workers throughout the agency, managers undermined the dual compensation plan necessary to implement the pay-for-knowledge plan (Shareef 1998). This is a common reaction by managers when they feel excluded from the new pay intervention. Interestingly, two years of new pay utilization appears to be the maximum amount of time that either group -- managers or workers -- can enjoy the benefits of new pay without creating feelings of pay inequity and dysfunctions in the organization.

Competency pay for managers should be an integral component of the strategic plan for agencies that target workers as the initial change lever in new pay interventions. Competency-based human resource systems differ from traditional systems because compensation is organized around the person rather than the job (Heneman and Ledford 1997) and work is described by knowledge, skills, and abilities of the person doing the task.

Heneman and Ledford (1997) outlined several characteristics of competencies: (1) they are portable since they are characteristic of the individual rather than the job; (2) they must be verifiable, an important characteristic for purposes of pay systems design; and (3) competencies enable superior performance but are not direct indicators of performance. This means that a competency pay system is not a complete pay system and some means of paying for performance (in addition to paying for competencies) is necessary.

Like other new pay concepts, competency pay is only appropriate in participative or high-involvement cultures. This compensation system is also appropriate where the organizational culture supports flexible workteams and knowledge-based results. Agencies that have not facilitated these types of cultural and redesign changes have little chance of successfully implementing competency-based pay for managers and other professionals.

VDOT is still mired in a "bureaucratic culture" so successfully implementing competency pay for managers is remote. Learning and operationalizing the competencies desired by the agency -- interpersonal influence, customer service orientation, and technical operations information -- would be relatively easy for managers to learn. However, VDOT's static organizational culture lends itself more to the traditional reward system that emphasizes fixed managerial work roles -- work that is measured through repetitive execution of tasks -- and little management discretion in work performance.

Many politicians and public administrators act as if new pay processes are simply symbolic public policies (Dye 1978). This type of thinking represents a congruency between traditional political and bureaucratic paradigms. Historically, public organizations were expected to be inefficient and higher taxes would subsidize that inefficiency.

However, the ground has shifted. Taxpayers now believe that governmental agencies can be more efficient and productive. Symbolic policies -- long on promises, but short on lasting results -- are no longer acceptable. If new pay processes and workplace democracy don't improve performance outcomes in public agencies, the calls for privatization and/or the contracting out of services will accelerate.

One way or the other, fundamental operating changes are coming to public organizations.

Implications

Nearly 30 years ago, Child (1973) concluded that size was the major predictor of decentralization. Size also appears to be the major determinant of whether a public agency targets the managerial group or workers as the new pay change lever. Smaller municipalities like Charlotte and College Station, Texas have implemented successful pay innovations by targeting workers and quickly diffusing the intervention through the ranks. Larger public agencies are unable to spread an innovation as quickly and probably should target managerial behavior as the pay change lever.

Most smaller agencies don't have a competency pay contingency for managers in their strategic plan. This is a major mistake. Growing managerial inequity issues (remember public managers have to simultaneously serve as change agents and day-to-day administrators) and poor alignment between pay and valued managerial competencies will eventually undermine the agency's strategic objectives.

Larger agencies like the USPS and VDOT acknowledge managerial behavior as a crucial change lever. However, the Postal Service did not link pay and diffusion as strategic goals causing the bonus pay plan to (1) remain a management perk and (2) create dissension with union members. Whenever managerial behavior is the lead change variable in a new pay intervention, the performance management process must tie administrative pay and diffusion of the pay plan as strategic objectives.

Although competency-based managerial pay was a strategic goal, VDOT simply did not implement the pay plan in a timely manner. Thus, the agency's administrators undermined the pay innovation. This is an important lesson for all stakeholders to remember -- the management team has to receive benefits from the pay innovation in the early stages of the intervention or they will become alienated from the process.

Moreover, neither USPS or VDOT planners recognized that bonus and skill-based pay would trigger cultural change in their organizations. Neither agency was prepared for that type of strategic change. Faced with the prospect of inadvertently creating a high-involvement work culture, administrators in both agencies employed traditional bureaucratic self-destructive behaviors that compromised efficiency improvements and political support.

The unethical behavior of USPS management on this, and other issues, has led a U.S. Postal Rate Commissioner to lead a public campaign calling for the privatization of the agency (Shareef 1999b). To many observers, the USPS seems totally resistant to strategic pay processes that decentralize and improve efficiency. The only solution, then, for USPS inefficiency (from this perspective) is free market competition.

Although size influences decentralization, a number of organizations utilizing new pay processes have successfully pushed decision-making down and developed decentralized operating units. The focus on strategic planning in innovative pay interventions must be on systems alignment with the new pay intervention. A strategic objective must be the linking of managerial compensation with decentralization.

Environmental scanning processes should monitor how other public agencies (and private sector organizations as well) have successfully aligned new pay interventions and decentralization processes. These scanning endeavors must also identify and solicit input, and feedback after diffusion, from political elites and community groups affected by new pay-triggered changes. Because of its many stakeholders, decentralization in public organizations is a complex internal and external dynamic.

Chapter 5

Improving the Relationship Between Public Administration Intellectuals and the Business Press: Two Areas of "Fit"

The media is often accused of having a liberal bias in the reporting of political news (Anderson 1992). This bias is thought to greatly influence the public's perceptions of leaders and the policies they espouse. Rarely, however, have organizational theorists considered how the business press shapes the consumer's (i.e., stakeholders) impressions of leaders (both public and private) and organizations.

Business writers determine how much will be used or ignored and also how information will be interpreted and given meaning in the constructed image of leaders and organizations (Chen and Meindl 1992). In theory, many possible constructions are possible. In practice, alternative constructions are likely to emerge from two value-preferences (Chen and Meindl 1991, 524):

- Antideterminism -- The antideterministic perspective is reflected in theories that suggest that the fates and fortunes of a firm can be understood in terms of the personal endowments of the leaders in charge. A more deterministic perspective suggests that the firms' performance is understood more in terms of the environmental and internal constraints facing management. A key difference in these two perspectives are the assumptions made regarding the extent to which managements are capable of exercising, through their unique endowments, control over unruly environments in the service of organization performance. For the antideterminist, the principal significance of a leader lies in the substantive actions and activities, which effectively isolate their firms from the vagaries of environment or use environment to the advantage of their firms in direct proportion to their abilities and skills.

- Professional Values and Ideologies -- News selection and treatment are not free from values and ideology. From the ideological hegemony perspective, the media is seen as part of the political system, specialized in formulating and distributing the ideology of the dominant social power. ... If news contains value and ideology, we will certainly find expressions in leader images constructed in the news. And since values and ideology are stable and enduring, news organizations will attempt to preserve the image of the leader who reflects the existing values and shapes future values of the national culture.

One of the most dominant values of the business press is a fixation with the "romance of leadership" notion. This belief, unifying both antideterminism and ideology, suggests that popular images of leadership are necessary to maintain stability in quickly changing environments:

> Whenever particular reconstructions emerge, their general themes must not diminish the significance of leadership as a way of understanding performance. The business press, with its antideterministic bent, makes an important contribution to that kind of reassurance. Just as buyers and sellers through their influence on supply and demand determine prices in the marketplace, writers and readers who traffic in images of leadership influence each other to determine how leaders are talked about and, in the end, how these images are systematically reconstructed to preserve leadership as a concept. In doing so, we rescue ourselves from the threats of a dangerous and capricious world and the disconcerting prospects of uncontrollable, if organized, human systems (Chen and Meindl 1991, 540).

Thus, antideterministic leaders are always involved in what Weick (1995) called ongoing sensemaking -- being thrown into complex situations which have no absolute starting points and forced to make and then revise provisional assumptions -- to bring apparent calm in a turbulent world. Known as cultural innovators in the leadership literature (Schein 1995), these leaders primary task is to communicate new values, facilitate change, and reassure nervous stakeholders when environmental challenges threaten the organization.

Nobody manifest this linkage between the press' construction of leader images and the personification of power, on a global level, than Federal Reserve Chairman Alan Greenspan. This results is what I call the "Greenspan Effect" -- the leader's ability to calm stakeholder anxiety during periods of crisis. For those who are good at accomplishing this task, the business press constructs favorable images. Moreover, positive reconstructions occur even in periods of performance declines.

At the national level, former U.S. Secretary of the Treasury Robert Rubin was the ultimate antideterministic public administrator. When he resigned from the top job at the Treasury on July 4, 1999, financial markets went into a tailspin, dropping 213 points before rebounding. This sudden drop was testimony of the confidence Rubin had developed on Wall Street because of his handling of the economy, especially his focus on deficit reduction. Falling deficits helped fuel a rising stock market and led to a cycle of borrowing and spending by business and consumers alike.

Time, Newsweek, U.S. News & World Reports, and the Wall Street Journal all acknowledged Rubin's antideterministic behaviors in bringing calm and stability to volatile national and international markets. Based on Chen and Meindl's (1991) findings, these positive press constructions will continue (i.e., reconstructions) for Rubin's successor (Larry Summers) even if the market took a serious downturn. The reason -- the need to protect the significance of leadership in the turbulent world of financial markets.

The business press' antideterministic and ideological values are capsuled by the comments of a USA Today business writer: "Rubin obviously feels confident in the recovery of the world financial system. He would not otherwise accept responsibility for subjecting the markets to a change in his office. No matter how justifiably confident he is in the ability of his successor to handle the job and transition, he would not be leaving the helm if he saw rough waters" (Henry 1999).

Deterministic Leaders

Conversely, the deterministic leader sees the leader's role as largely symbolic, primarily concerned with preserving institutional integrity (Terry 1995). Organizational change is viewed as incremental and evolutionary rather than constant and turbulent. Here, environmental turbulence is thought to be predictable and threats to the organization can be handled with traditional management strategies like downsizing and autocratic work cultures.

Retired Los Angeles Police Chief Darryl Gates is an example of a public sector "deterministic" leader. Current Virginia Governor Gilmore is another.

Furthermore, deterministic views minimize human influence over events occurring in the environment. Change is thought to be driven by impersonal forces, not human interpretations of events. As the prominent conservative economist Thomas Sowell (1995, 124) notes, the wisdom, will, and commitment of individual leaders have little causal impact on organization outcomes:

> Systemic causation operates in a wide spectrum of circumstances, whether in the world of human nature or human societies. Vegetation on a mountainside may fall into a pattern, not because any of the trees or plants sought to produce such a pattern, but because different heights favor the survival of different species. Even where human violation is involved, the overall pattern that emerges may not reflect anyone's violation. The Dow Jones average may stand at 4086, not because anyone planned it that way, but because that was the net result of innumerable people seeking their own individual advantage on the particular stock they were trading.

Determinism and Public Administration

The field of public administration, both the academy and practitioners, is often viewed by the business press as deterministic. Certainly, the writings of particular scholars (Goodsell 1985; Wilson 1989; Terry 1995) have contributed to this image. While these writings represent only a fraction of the scholarship on public sector change, they do reinforce a traditional idea of public organizations that operated in less turbulent environments.

In fact, much of the academic literature has focused on describing the bureaucratic nature of public agencies (Goodsell 1985; Wilson 1989), not on transforming these organizations. Public sector managers, seen as ineffective and threatened by change, are viewed in the media as actors whose main goal is to defend the status quo (Terry 1995).

Because of the perceived incongruency between the antideterministic values of the business press and traditional public administration values, scholars and practitioners in the field are often excluded from new pay strategic planning processes. For example, when the former Governor of Virginia created a task force to improve state government, public administration theorists and managers were excluded. Importantly, there was no demand from media elites that they be included on the task force.

How do public administration intellectuals and practitioners facilitate a better relationship with the business press? Certainly, one of the best ways is to exhibit antideterministic behaviors concerning agency change and efficiency processes. Current Houston Mayor Lee Brown offers a case study example of bringing "fit" between public service and business press values. As a result, he has received positive image construction from both the local and national press.

Altruistic Democracy: The Link Pin
Between Public Administration and
Business Press Values

The Chen and Meindl research has also reported a unique press value associated with public sector leader image construction -- altruistic democracy. This value-preference suggests that politicians, officials, and the system of democracy are expected to be efficient, honest, and dedicated to acting in the public interest. These values are consistent with traditional norm-based (e.g., civic duty and public interest) and affective (e.g., self-sacrifice) public service motivations identified by Perry and Wise (1990).

Public administrators who exhibit antideterministic value preferences and altruistic democracy traits receive the most positive constructions and reconstructions from the media. When Lee Brown became the Police Commissioner of New York City, he introduced a strategic redesign effort to reduce crime through the community policing concept (Webber 1991). The change plan called for a shift from a bureaucratic command and control system to a high-involvement culture. The hiring, appraisal, training and reward systems were redesigned to "fit" with the agency's strategic objective -- decentralized community policing to reduce crime in New York City.

Commissioner Brown's community policing approach was viewed by the media as a vital public interest issue. Because of his previous successes (i.e., reducing violent crime) as the police chief in Atlanta and Houston, the press essentially saw Brown as fulfilling his civic duty when he took the NYC Commissioner's position. New pay processes, designed to hire a better-educated and more diverse police force, were supported by those who shape public images and opinion.

The upshot of the Lee Brown story is that violent crime dropped dramatically in NYC during the 1990s. Community policing was given the credit for this reduction. Yet, other factors that influence crime --

the leveling off of men in the 18-26 year old bracket, the waning use of crack cocaine, longer incarcerations for those who commit violent crime, and a booming economy -- are discounted as causal factors for crime reduction in NYC. Only Commissioner Brown's leadership (antideterministic) and community policing (altruistic democracy) are offered by the press to the public as reasons for a safer New York.

The altruistic democracy value plays such a linking function between public administrators and the business press that when it is abandoned, an incongruency with press value-orientations occurs with resulting negative image and agency constructions. When Howard Safir assumed the NYC Commissioner's position in the mid-1990s, he maintained most elements of Brown's community policing concept but also implemented more militaristic-style units for crime prevention. Brown publicly criticized the use of these aggressive "street crimes units" for operating under the guise of community policing.

Although crime is dramatically down in NYC, Safir has been vilified in the local and national press for several shootings and cases of police brutality. On Thursday, September 23, 1999, the popular PBS show, The News Hour, raised the question of whether "street crimes units" were an asset or liability to law enforcement. The more high-profile cases from New York were discussed.

The two panelists disagreed. Bernard Parks, current Los Angeles Police Chief, thought the units were necessary but needed closer supervision. Joseph McNamara, former Police Chief of San Jose, CA believed that the militaristic approach to policing had no place on American streets. Though not present, Police Commissioner Safir received negative construction(s) from the moderator for (1) not controlling his department and (2) for violating another element of altruistic democracy -- creating impersonal, intrusive governmental units. The same type of negative construction of Commissioner Safir's leadership style, and the NYC Police Department, occurred during an October 25, 1999 interview with Harper Magazine's John MacArthur on C-Span's Washington Journal.

Public agency transformations, driven by new pay processes, will receive positive image constructions from the press as long as there is congruency between the leader/agency and the value-preference of the media. If public administration actors want to be involved in the strategic planning and decision-making processes that affect their agencies, they must understand this relationship. Failure to do so leads to the type of exclusion described earlier by Roberts concerning Governor Allen's change task force.

For the business press, the preservation of the leadership concept as a process of reassuring nervous stakeholders in a turbulent world is priority. While other factors may well explain agency performance -- as the Brown case illustrates -- they are ignored because of the antideterministic bent of the press. Sowell (1995) calls this phenomena "the irrelevance of empirical evidence" in public policymaking. There is some truth in his statement.

Yet, it is also true that when organized systems are under threat and collapse, there have to be leaders available to "make sense" of the situation. Otherwise, there is disaster. Weick (1996, 148) found that when "a role system collapses among people for whom trust, honesty, and self-respect are developed, then new options, such as mutual adoption, blind imitation of creative solutions, and trusting compliance are created."

Furthermore, Weick (1995) contends that the belief that someone trustworthy is at the "helm" is often the major determinant of organizational success and failure. The business press cherishes that value as well. As public administration scholars and managers, we need to better understand the dynamics of impression management when introducing new pay processes into agency life.

Implications

The value preferences of "business writers" suggest that anti-deterministic leaders like Robert Rubin and Lee Brown will get more favorable image constructions than deterministic leaders. These leaders inspire confidence in stakeholders during periods of environmental crisis. This despite factors that appear beyond the control of the personal qualities of the leader. Indeed, on-going social constructions (and reconstructions) of reality by the leader seem to be the catalyst for superior organizational performance in times of turbulence.

From this perspective, the antideterministic leader actually constructs social reality through his/her energetic, confident, and motivated response to environmental turbulence. Bold leadership shapes -- rather than responds to -- emerging environmental turbulence. For example, Lee Brown's community policing concept -- with its emphasis on police mobility and visibility as a deterrent to crime -- may have actually been the stimulus for NYC's strong economic growth in recent years.

The perception of personal safety based on police visibility -- even in a city that still records 1,000 homicides annually -- has lured businesses and tourists back to New York. Because of perceived improved police-community relations spawned by community policing, criminals are unlikely to commit brazen crimes for fear of being turned in by their neighbors or other citizens. In effect, NYC appears safer because business people, visitors, and criminals believe that law enforcement is virtually omnipresent.

In the social construction of reality the plausibility of policy (as opposed to its accuracy) is the greater determinant of organizational and societal outcomes. For instance, since it is plausible for the citizens (both law-abiding and criminal) of New York City to believe that the community policing concept makes more officers available for crime prevention and assistance, the city (in reality) becomes safer. Plausibility is a value-preference that both antideterministic leaders and the business press recognize.

Weick (1995, 113), in explaining belief-driven processes of social constructions of reality, writes that "First, there are beliefs embedded in frames such as ideologies or paradigms, that's what people notice and how events unfold. Beliefs affect how events unfold when they produce a self-fulfilling prophecy. In matters of sensemakng, believing is seeing. To believe is to notice selectively."

Antideterminism and organization sensemaking processes are based on what Morgan (1985) called "circles of causality" where A influences B but B also influences A. Conversely, deterministic thinking is more logical and linear and ignores the ideologies of emotionally changed beliefs, values, and norms that bind people together. Deterministic perspectives discount the emotionally-driven attributes (i.e., attribution theory) that followers bestow on leaders and that leaders, in turn, use to shape social reality. Thus, Terry (1995) and Sowell (1995) ignore the role of leaders (and the press) in constructing emotionally-changed public policies that directly influence the outcomes of organized human systems.

If public administration theorists and managers, as opposed to business professors and consultants, are going to be included in strategic planning change, their value orientations will have to become more congruent with the values and ideologies of the media. This perceived ideological incongruency leads to the exclusion of those who best understand the values and motivations inherent in public institutions. It appears that altruistic democracy provides an umbrella for linking the press' antideterministic ideology with traditional public administration values.

The principle of altruistic democracy calls for the creation of small, humanistic governmental units that serve the public. This is true whether we're speaking of anti-crime units in New York City or customer service operations in the Virginia Department of Transportation. Public sector leaders who are successful in initially creating such units have often been unsuccessful in preventing them from reverting back to impersonal, bureaucratic units focused solely on efficiency outcomes.

When this occurs, it creates a "feeding frenzy" in the media that features calls for either business (1) leaders or (2) academics to rescue the incompetent public manager. This cycle occurs so frequently that it is predictable. The only way for those involved in the public administration enterprise to mitigate this established pattern of dysfunctional behavior is to align values and orientations with those who both construct leader/organizational images and shape public opinion -- the business press.

Chapter 6

New Pay and Organization Learning

The previous chapter closed with the admonition that public administration theorists and practitioners must learn to develop congruency between public administration values and those of the media. Part of the difficulty in achieving this "fit" is that bureaucratic actors tend to see learning as a single-loop dynamic. Single-loop learning suggests that organizational inefficiencies or dysfunctions are related to a departure from established procedures or goals (Argyris and Schon 1978). Effectiveness is reestablished based on how quickly the organization returns to its traditional practices and goals. This type of learning is more closely related to incremental change processes described earlier by Nadler and Tushman (1990).

As it relates to the process of aligning public administration values and those of the business press, a single-loop learning process that returns leadership behavior back to bureaucratic/deterministic behaviors totally undermines any "fit" with media values. Indeed, none of the new pay change processes discussed in this text lend themselves to single-looping learning processes. The conceptual misunderstanding by public administrators of strategic change and double-loop learning processes have doomed most interventions from the start.

Double-loop learning occurs when "... The routines and goals of the agency are no longer adequate for the problems faced, returning to them only makes the problems worse. This is where double-loop learning enters -- learning not only that the organization is off course, but that its very conception of how to reach its goal is outmolded and must be replaced (Gortner, Mahler, and Nicholson 1997, 117)." As a strategic change concept, new pay falls into the double-loop learning framework.

Senge (1990) outlines five disciplines necessary to create the learning organization. They are systems thinking, personal mastery, mental models, building shared values, and team learning. Like Agyris and Schon's double-loop learning concept, Senge's approach calls for the radical redesign of the organization's systems and structures that are thought to reinforce patterns of learning behavior. Obviously, both approaches see systems redesign and alignment as being essential to organizational learning. Moreover, both approaches see open communication systems, as a means of facilitating feedback, as being key to the learning process.

Organization Learning and Rewards

Vicarious learning theory offers a more behaviorist construct to learning and change (Bandura 1986). In this context, the term operant condition describes the environment in which behavior(s) are learned and reinforced. Operant behaviors are determined by several factors: positive reinforcement, negative reinforcement, extinction, and punishment.

Bandura found that "leadership modeling" influences subordinate learning. He reported that if the observer sees certain behavior succeed for others, it increases the tendency to behave in a like manner. In other words, the observer has learned, based on the experience of a relevant other, that particular behaviors lead to success. If the observer sees the behavior of a relevant other punished, however, it reduces the likelihood of that behavior being repeated by the observer.

For purposes of this discussion, it is important to note that Bandura's research shows that rewarded modeling is more effective than modeling alone in fostering organizational learning. Additionally, the modeling and rewarding practices of subordinates by supervisors constitute an organization's strongest vicarious learning process (Bowers and Seashore 1966).

Double-loop learning processes and SBP have been successfully implemented in Baltimore County. County Executive Ruppersberger "models" the behaviors he wants demonstrated throughout the organization -- and he rewards those who exhibit those behaviors. The appraisal, training, communications, and compensation systems have been redesigned to reinforce high-involvement activities. Workers throughout the organization learn vicariously that strategic behaviors are desired and rewarded through increased pay, promotion, and other forms of recognition.

Learning and the Skills Package

The Winter Commission (1993) and Roberts (1994) call for learning government through enhanced training and education. Five steps are outlined: restoring employee training and education budgets; creating a new skills package for all employees; basing pay increases on skills, not time in position; insisting on a new kind of problem-solving manager; and encouraging a new style of labor-management communication. The skills package would also include competencies in team building, communication, employee involvement, cultural awareness, and quality.

The learning/skills package articulated by The Winter Commission and Roberts are predicated on a "new pay" system -- and double-loop learning processes.

Learning and Business Education

Another type of organization learning focuses on the need for workers in high-performance government to possess a broad understanding of how the agency works. That is, employees need business education (Lawler 1992). Keeping workers informed of the constant challenges the organization faces creates a "shared reality" that both the employee and worker must understand if the agency is to reach its strategic goals.

Research recently conducted at the University of Virginia's Center for Public Service reveals that employers have grown increasingly intolerant of workers who show little interest in the "business side" of organizational life (Martin and Carrier 1998). Yet, very little of this business knowledge becomes available to workers until a crisis threatens the organization. In public organizations, this often occurs when elected officials announce that a traditional service is being outsourced or privatized because a business firm can perform the service more efficiently.

There are several instances where good business education has taken place in government institutions. City government in Indianapolis is a good example. Initially, the city hired a large accounting firm to teach administrators and employees activity-based cost accounting (Goldsmith 1997). Employees then helped determine which services should be outsourced and which should be retained since they (city employees) were cost-effective at handling these services because of skills and specialization.

The USPS variable pay program is driven by the concept of EVA (Economic Value Added). This economic concept measures how well the agency uses its resources and rewards employees on that measurement. A booklet published by the USPS (1997, 3) explains EVA by stating: "EVA creates value only when net operating income exceeds the cost of capital we use. To drive EVA upward, we must increase profitable revenues, reduce expenses, and use employee capital more efficiently."

Business education and training are mandatory for any postal employee participating in this variable pay program. Concepts like net operating income, capital, cost of capital, and the EVA formula all have to be learned by employees before implementation and diffusion. Understanding market share, how to improve it, and enhanced financial performance are the centerpiece(s) linking business education and the new pay process in the USPS.

In Baltimore County, the business learning process begins for employees involved in gainsharing through intensive training in the TQM and team-building strategies. Teams later develop cost-saving ideas, evaluate these ideas, determine their feasibility, and package them for presentation to the County Executive. The strategic goal is for the team to create more efficient government by bringing specialized knowledge, insights, and experience to the problem-solving process. Gainsharing provides an economic incentive for employees to increase their problem-solving knowledge, thereby creating a more efficient organization.

The "business" of gainsharing is important to Baltimore County employees as well. Director of Personnel Antony Sharbaugh believes that knowledge gained through gainsharing has reversed the outsourcing trend and helped employees reestablish a sense of job security. As stakeholders in the government enterprise, he notes that "gainshare" employees better understand how waste and poor quality directly affect their security and income. Because of this business knowledge, workers know an efficient government operation means greater incomes and a decreased chance of downsizing or contracting out work.

Cost-accounting practices like those used in Indianapolis and the USPS' EVA plan require extensive business education and training. Less complicated new pay processes like winsharing in Virginia's Higher Education System are relatively unstructured. It is in this environment that a more vicarious learning dynamic, based on leadership modeling, takes place as academic units compare after-budget spending practices.

If a Dean of one college restricts spending and another doesn't, faculty members learn "vicariously" that a disincentive for efficiency exists. Consequently, faculty members in these academic units will "top-out" the spending of their budgets during the fiscal year because no economic incentive for organizational efficiency is forthcoming. Obviously, new pay, leadership modeling, and vicarious learning must all synergize to facilitate business education.

Implications

New pay processes are strategic change interventions that "fit" with double-loop, but not single-loop, learning processes. Moreover, three types of organizational learning – vicarious, skill enhancement, and business education – are associated with new pay interventions. These types of organization learning should be inherent features of a high-performance government culture since they emphasize the desirability of control through shared understanding of how the organization works, what its goals and objectives are, and the values it stands for (Lawler 1984).

Public sector leaders often overlook the importance of "modeling" and rewarding the types of behavior they want to see exhibited. Or maybe not. Modeling and rewarding processes have always been aligned to promote bureaucratic culture and values; consequently, the issue of inconsistent modeling/rewarding practices appears to occur only during paradigmatic cultural change.

Pfeffer (1998) reported that many senior business managers acknowledge the need for this type of "fit" but found organizational cultures/traditions significant impediments to creating alignment during the change process. Congruent modeling/rewarding practices by the leaders make a dramatic statement about what behaviors will be accepted in the high-involvement culture. Most often, however, the leader seeks to maintain the status quo.

This was evident during the restructuring of Virginia's Higher Education System in the early 1990s. One of the goals was improved employee relations based on employee involvement. Although Governor George Allen talked about cooperation between administrators and faculty, his management style was clearly autocratic. Because of this type of management culture, it was predicted that no "new pay" intervention would be successfully implemented during his administration (Shareef 1994c).

The non-aligned higher education reward system did not provide incentives for administrators to facilitate a cooperative decision-making mechanism with faculty during the restructuring process. The reward system only compensated administrators for short-term cost reductions. By watching appointments and promotions, administrators quickly learned that rewards were only forthcoming to managers who exhibited bureaucratic behaviors.

This compensation was not only financial. Higher education bureaucrats also learned vicariously that greater autocratic power and influence awaited those who modeled the Governor's behaviors:

> Further, under this structure, administrative merchants not only have almost exclusive control over important changes in the system, but over how and when they will be implemented. Most important, their control over such decisions have given them comparable power over the distribution of the costs and benefits associated with them, allowing them to minimize the costs of these changes to themselves and to other stakeholders whose interest they chose to protect at the expense of those they perceive to be less important/powerful in the system (Birecree and Woolley 1997, 114).

The same type of vicarious learning is taking place in the current round of higher education restructuring in Virginia. Governor Allen's successor, James Gilmore, promised university presidents autonomy in the restructuring process. However, he is clearly attempting to micromanage the process from Richmond (Hebel 2000). Lower level education officials are "learning" vicariously from his modeling and rewarding practices -- despite his rhetoric.

The Winter Commission (1993) warned that micromanaging of the change process by a government official would kill the move toward decentralization or high-involvement. It clearly has in Virginia. Most of the university presidents are now simply trying to "outlast" the Gilmore Administration which ends in 2002.

Many public administrators are surprised by the use of business education as a learning instrument in governmental agencies. Yet, public agency leaders understand that they operate in very competitive environments. Moreover, they know that public workers must understand the competitive nature of their "business" and employ strategies to remain competitive.

Complex valuations like the USPS' EVA system can make the understanding of value-added business education too complex, thus blurring the alignment between new pay and productivity. This may be one of the reasons it has not been pushed down from the management ranks in the USPS. However, value-added education can be operationalized in a much less complicated manner.

For example, the University of Tennessee's William Sanders has developed value-added tests that assess teacher effectiveness (USA Today Editorial Page 2000). These variables are thought to be the key to a student's academic success. The tests are used to provide teachers feedback on their weaknesses. The Denver, CO School District is using this value-added approach and rewarding teachers who boost test scores with a $2,500 bonus.

Baltimore County has a simplified business education and new pay plan. So does the American Red Cross where tentative plans call for linking value-added business education to improve customer service. Bonus pay will be used to reward customer service units that attain 96% customer satisfaction approval ratings. Non-profit leaders, like their business sector colleagues, have to always remember that business strategy drives performance with new pay systems the mediating variable.

The clearer the employees' vision between strategy (business education), new pay, and performance, the more likely the agency's learning objectives will be achieved.

Chapter 7

Conclusions: Privatization, New Pay, and the Future of Public Organizations

The previous chapters have discussed strategies for implementing new pay processes in public organizations. Hopefully, a better understanding of the role that new pay interventions can play in transforming political institutions, rather than business enterprises, now exists. At the end of the day, however, the reader may question whether these transformations are really that important.

I think they are. Without improved productivity and operating efficiencies, the drift toward greater privatization and outsourcing will accelerate. Conservative politicians, taxpayers, and the media will lead this push. Public sector workers clearly see this pattern developing (Shareef 1998) while many public administration theorists and managers tend to underestimate the potential impact of the privatization movement.

The recent comments of Indianapolis Mayor Steven Goldsmith (1997, 121) concerning the privatization of public agencies should give skeptics reason to rethink their position on this issue:

> ... I was asked whether there were any limits on what services could be privatized. Exaggerating to make a point, I said that city government could be run with a mayor, a police chief, a planning director, a purchasing director, and a handful of contract monitors. ... The point remains, however, that while government must ensure the provision of certain services, there is no reason why government must produce those services.

New pay interventions offer a powerful counterweight to the privatization/outsourcing movement. Yet, as was noted earlier, these pay innovations must be permanent and not merely a "passing fad". Regrettably, public administrators have often used these change interventions to offset threats of privatization. Once this threat was reduced by the half-hearted implementation of new pay processes, agency heads usually reverted back to bureaucratic practices and norms.

The privatization of public schools in the United States provides a micro illustration of what happens when governmental leaders don't take cultural change processes seriously. Some schools in Baltimore, MD and Hartford, CT are fully privatized. Charter schools are legal in Virginia and other states. School vouchers are being utilized in Wisconsin, Ohio, and Florida (Shareef 2000a). Because of their success, these policy initiatives now enjoy wide public support.

Public school officials nationwide ignored these environmental threats until they gained taxpayer and political support. Now, they are playing "performance" catch-up by using new pay plans. It is questionable, however, if these plans can mitigate the gains enjoyed by movements like school vouchers. One reason is that public schools have to share resources with the voucher program. Every dollar used to administer a voucher plan is a dollar less available for a bonus or value-added gainshare incentive plan for teachers.

Peter Senge (1990) argues that there is a gap between cause and effect in the organizational learning process. That is, while change is always occurring, it is slow and incremental. Consequently, institutional leaders only perceive a stable environment. By the time the leadership team recognizes the environmental challenge, they are already at a competitive (and for public agencies a political) disadvantage.

Thurow (1996, 8) calls this process "punctuated equilibrium" -- a period where everything is in flux, disequilibrium becomes the norm, and uncertainty reigns. Both he and Senge argue convincingly that the ignoring of these environmental movements are the primary cause for organizational demise and eventual death. This type of slow demise is exactly where many public organizations find themselves at the beginning of the 21st century.

Despite political proclamations, privatization/outsourcing are not a panacea for what ails public agencies. For example, many universities have outsourced day-to-day operations and maintenance of on-campus buildings to private companies. However, these arrangements have not proven successful largely because of conflict between private sector managers and public sector union employees. In this regard, the Vice President for University Services at George

Mason University has stated, "It isn't just me or my office or my staff, it has to be a university commitment to make these kinds of contracts work. You need help from the materials-management department, the legal-affairs office, the president, the buildings and grounds crew. Everyone has to adopt this mindset" (Van Der Nerf 2000, A39).

This type of cooperation is difficult to get when union members view outsourcing as a way to break the union. In fact, Pfeffer (1998) suggests that public policy be used to (1) foster the building of more cooperative labor relations, (2) encourage training and the diffusion of better management practices, and (3) facilitate the implementation of high performance work arrangements. He makes these recommendations because the market has failed to produce best management practices in the workforce. Thus, Pfeffer believes the best option for improving labor relations and creating high performance cultures in American organizations will come through the public policy process -- not through marketplace dynamics.

As I write this in the Spring of 2000, the Virginia Department of Transportation has just announced that it will end SBP on June 30th of this year. Several reasons for abandoning this pay innovation were given: in many districts, only maintenance personnel were covered under the plan. Their pay increases created tensions with workers whom the plan was never diffused to; there was never a redesigned evaluation system to test workers who were given points for skill attainment(s) by their supervisors. A state audit revealed that many workers were assigned points, and given pay increases, for skills they did not process; and many workers were making more money than their supervisors.

All of the pathologies that plagued the VDOT SBP program were related to strategic redesign issues. In effect, this was a poorly conceived new pay intervention that has cost the taxpayers of Virginia millions of dollars. Traditional public administration scholars will point to this as the latest example of the incompatibility of new pay concepts and public institutions. More significantly, the beliefs of conservative politicians, taxpayers, interest groups, and media elites that public organizations should either be privatized or dismembered through outsourcing will be reinforced.

Mayor Goldsmith's comments represent a manifesto for the privatization of public sector institutions. However, new pay advocates believe that these processes can neutralize this challenge by improving performance, efficiency, and worker quality-of-worklife while simultaneously maintaining traditional public administration values and motivations.

The proper utilization of new pay interventions may simply be the best way to salvage the "uniqueness" of public organizations.

REFERENCES

Adams, J. Stacy. "Inequity in Social Exchange." In Psychological Foundations in Organizational Behavior, edited by Barry Shaw, 110-124. Santa Monica: Goodyear Publishing, 1977.

Agim, Innocent. 1994. Political Patronage, Merit Principles, and the Genesis of Merit. Ph.D. diss., Virginia Polytechnic Institute and State University.

Anderson, Martin. 1992. Imposters in the Temple: American Intellectuals Are Destroying Our Universities and Cheating Our Students of their Future. New York: Simon and Schuster.

Argyris, Chris and Schon, Donald. 1978. Organization Learning: A Theory of Action Perspective. Reading, MA: Addison-Wesley.

Bandura, Albert. 1986. Social Foundations of Thought and Action: A Social Cognitive Theory. Englewood Cliffs: Prentice Hall.

Barringer, Melissa and Milkovich, George. 1998. "A Theoretical Exploration of the Adoption and Design of Flexible Benefits Plan: A Case of Human Resource Innovation." Academy of Management Review 23: 305-324.

Bennis, Warren. 1989. On Becoming A Leader. Reading, MA: Addison-Wesley.

Bennis, Warren and Nanus, Burt. 1985. Leaders. New York: Harper & Row.

Birecree, Adrienne and Woolley, Douglas. 1997. "Restructuring the Virginia State System of Higher Education." International Contributions to Labour Studies 7: 97-117.

Bowers, David and Seashore, Stanley. 1966. "Predicting Organizational Effectiveness with a Four-Factor Theory of Leadership." Administrative Science Quarterly: 11: 250-263.

Chen, Chan and Meindl, James. "The Construction of Leadership Images in the Popular Press: The Case of Don Burr and People Express." Administrative Science Quarterly 33:521-551.

Child, John. 1973. "Predicting and Understanding Organization Structure." Administrative Science Quarterly 18: 168-185.

Department of Public Works - Arlington, VA. 1985. "Skill-Based Pay Pilot Project: Building Skills, Building Ownership, Creating High Performance.": 1-42.

Dessler, Gary. 1986. Organization Theory: Integrating Structure and Behavior. Englewood Cliffs: Prentice Hall.

Dye, Thomas. 1978. Understanding Public Policy (3rd). Englewood Cliffs: Prentice Hall.

Goldsmith, Stephen. 1997. "Can Business Really Do Business with Government?" Harvard Business Review 75: 110-121.

Goodsell, Charles. 1985. The Case for Bureaucracy (2nd). Chatham, NJ: Chatham House.

Gortner, Harold, Mahler, Julianne, and Nicholson, Jeanne Bell. 1997. Organization Theory: A Public Perspective (2nd). Ft. Worth: Harcourt Brace College Publishers.

Hebel, Sara. "Virginia Plan Offers Fiscal Stability, but the Attached Strings Worry Colleges." The Chronicle of Higher Education. 18 February 2000, A42-44.

Heneman, Robert and Ledford, Gerald. 1997. "Competency Pay for Professionals and Managers in Business: A Review and Implications for Teachers." Center for Effective Organizations - University of Southern California (Marshall School of Business): 1-19.

Henry, David. "Rubin Move May Have Long-Term Effect." USA Today, 13 May 1999, B1-2.

Huse, Edgar and Cummings, Thomas. 1989. Organization Development and Change (4th). St. Paul: West Publishing.

Ingraham, Patricia and Romzek, Barbara. "Preface." In New Paradigms for Government: Issues for the Changing Public Service, edited by Patricia Ingraham and Barbara Romzek, XIII-XVII. San Francisco: Jossey-Bass, 1994.

Kane, Amy. "Postal Workers Picket for Better Contract." The Roanoke Times, 10 June 1999, p. B3.

Kanter, Rosabeth Moss. 1983. The Change Masters: Innovation and Entrepreneurship in the American Corporation. New York: Touchstone Books.

Kaufman, Herbert. 1981. The Administrative Behavior of Federal Bureau Chiefs. Washington, DC: Brookings Institution.

Klein, Janice. 1984. "Why Supervisors Resist Employee Involvement." Harvard Business Review 62: 87-95.

Lawler, Edward. 1998. "Creating Effective Pay Systems for Teams." Center for Effective Organizations - University of Southern California (Marshall School of Business): 1-26.

_____. 1995. "Strategic Human Resources Management: An Idea Whose Time Has Come." Center for Effective Organizations - University of Southern California (Marshall School of Business): 1-17 .

_____. 1992. The Ultimate Advantage: Creating the High Involvement Organization. San Francisco: Jossey-Bass.

_____. 1990. Strategic Pay: Aligning Organizational Strategies and Pay Systems. San Francisco: Jossey Bass.

_____. 1987. "Pay for Performance: A Strategic Analysis." Center for Effective Organizations - University of Southern California (Marshall School of Business): 1-74.

_____. 1986. High-Involvement Management: Participative Strategies for Improving Organizational Performance. Jossey-Bass: San Francisco.

_____. 1984. "The New Pay." Center for Effective Organizations - University of Southern California (Marshall School of Business): 1-15.

Ledford, Gerald. 1998. "Designing Nimble Reward Systems." Center for Effective Organizations - University of Southern California (Marshall School of Business): 1-21

Lindblom, Charles. 1977. Politics and Markets. New York: Basic Books.

Martin, Julia and Carrier, Achsah. 1998 (April). "Virginia's Changing Workplace in the 21st Century." Weldon Cooper Center for Public Service - University of Virginia, 1-7.

Miller, James C. III. 1990. "A Critique of the Case Against Privatization of the United States Postal Service." Center for Study of Public Choice - George Mason University: 1-10.

Morhman, Allen and Mohrman, Susan. 1997. "Managing Performance for Organizational Change and Learning." Center for Effective Organizations - University of Southern California (Marshall School of Business): 1-38.

Mohrman, Susan and Lawler, Edward. 1988. "Participative Managerial Behavior and Organizational Change." Center for Effective Organizations - University of Southern California (Marshall School of Business): 1-28.

Mohrman, Susan, Mohrman, Allen, and Tenkasi, Ramkrishnan. 1996. "The Discipline of Organization Design." Center for Effective Organizations - University of Southern California (Marshall School of Business): 1-17.

Morgan, Gareth. 1986. Images of Organizations. Thousand Oaks: Sage Publications.

Nadler, David and Tushman, Michael. 1990. "Beyond the Charismatic Leader: Leadership and Change." California Management Review 32: 77-95.

_____. 1989. "Organization Frame Bending: Principles of Managing Orientation." Academy of Management Executive 3: 194-205.

_____. 1980. "A Diagnostic Model for Organization Behavior." In Perspectives on Behavior, edited by J. R. Hackman, Edward Lawler, and Lyman Porter, 85-100. New York: McGraw-Hill.

Office of Personnel-Baltimore County, MD. 1997. "Gainsharing in Baltimore County.": 1-5.

Oregon Department of Transportation (Salem, OR). 1995. "Self-Directed Highway Maintenance Teams: Experiences and Lessons Learned During the First Five Years, 1990-1995.": 1-39.

Pearce, Jone, Stevenson, William, and Perry, James. 1985. "Management Compensation Based on Organizational Performance: A Time Series Analysis of the Effects of Merit Pay." Academy of Management Journal 28: 261-278.

Pearson, Sidney. 1998. Herbert Crowly: Progressive Democracy (A New Introduction). New Brunswick: Transaction Publishers.

Perry, James. "Revitalizing Employee Ties with Public Organizations." In New Paradigms for Government: Issues for the Changing Public Service, edited by Patricia Ingraham and Barbara Romzek, 191-214. San Francisco: Jossey-Bass, 1994.

_____. "Compensation, Merit Pay, and Motivation." In Public Personnel Administration: Problems and Prospects, edited by Steven Hays and Richard Kearney, 104-114. Englewood Cliffs: Prentice Hall, 1990.

Perry, James and Kraemer, Kenneth. "The Roots of Public Management." In Public Management: The Essential Readings, edited by J. Steven Ott, Albert Hyde, and Jay Shafritz, 5-9. Chicago: Lyceum Books/Nelson-Hill Publishers, 1991.

Perry, James and Wise, Lois. 1990. "The Motivational Bases of Public Service." Public Administration Review 50: 367-373.

Pfeffer, Jeffrey. 1998. The Human Equation: Building Profits by Putting People First. Cambridge: Harvard Business School.

Platt, Rodney. 1997. "How Gainsharing Can Work in the Public Sector." American Compensation Association News. February: 18-21.

Posner, Bruce and Rothstein, Lawrence. 1994. "Reinventing the Business of Government: An Interview with Change Catalyst David Osborne." Harvard Business Review 72: 133-143.

Rainey, Hal. "Rethinking Public Personnel Administration." In New Paradigms for Government: Issues for the Changing Public Service," edited by Patricia Ingraham and Barbara Romzek, 115-140. San Francisco: Jossey-Bass, 1994.

_____. "On the Uniqueness of Public Organizations." In The State of Public Bureaucracies, edited by Larry Hill, 111-140. Armonk, NY: M.E. Sharpe, 1992.

Risher, Howard. 1998. "Can Gainsharing Help to Reinvent Government?" Public Management 10: 17-21.

The Roanoke Times, 27 December 1997, "Big Profits Deliver An Attitude Adjustment: Incentive Bonuses Help Improve Service," A7.

Roberts, Deborah. 1995a (June/July). "Delivering on Democracy: High Performance Government for Virginia." Weldon Cooper Center for Public Service - University of Virginia, 1-11.

_____. 1995b (October/November). "Creating High Performance Government in Virginia: Norfolk's Experiences." Weldon Cooper Center for Public Service - University of Virginia, 1-7.

_____ 1994 (January). "Reinventing Government Virginia Style." Weldon Cooper Center for Public Service - University of Virginia, 1-8.

Schein, Edgar. 1985. Organizational Culture and Leadership. San Francisco: Jossey-Bass.

Schuster, Jay and Zingheim, Patricia. 1992. The New Pay: Linking Employee and Organizational Performance. New York: Lexington Books.

Senge, Peter. 1990. The Fifth Discipline: The Art and Practice of the Learning Organization. New York: Doubleday.

Silverman, David. 1971. The Theory of Organizations. New York: Basic Books.

Slater, Phillip and Bennis, Warren. 1990. "Democracy is Inevitable." Harvard Business Review 68: 167-176.

Shareef, Reginald. 2000a. "Educational Vouchers: Educational Wave of the Future." The Roanoke Times Online Service (www.roanoke. com/shareef), 27 March 2000, 1-5.

_____. 2000b. "Roanoke Public Schools New Pay Plan Makes for Good Strategic Policy." The Roanoke Times Online Service, (www.roanoke.com/shareef), 21 February 2000, 1-5.

_____. 1999a. "Why They Go Postal at the Postal Service, or VDOT, for that Matter." The Roanoke Times Online Service (www.roanoke.com/shareef), 6 December 1999, 1-5.

_____. 1999b. "Why They Will Continue to Go 'Postal' at the Postal Service." The Roanoke Times Online Service (www.roanoke.com/shareef), 13 December 1999, 1-4.

_____. 1998. "A Midterm Case Study of Skill-Based Pay in the Virginia Department of Transportation." Review of Public Personnel Administration 18: 5-22.

_____. 1997. "A Popperian View of Change in Innovative Organizations." Human Relations 50: 655-670.

_____. 1994a. "An Innovative Idea: Skill-Based Pay in the Public Sector." Review of Public Personnel Administration 14: 60-74.

_____. 1994b. "Subsystem Congruence: A Strategic Change Model for Public Organizations." Administration and Society 25: 489-517.

_____. 1994c. "Rewarding Skills: Reinvent Pay Plan for Government." The Roanoke Times, 7 April 1994, A12.

_____. 1993. "Understanding Strategic Transformations in Public Organizations." In Research in Public Administration, Volume 2, edited by James Perry, 167-189. Greenwich: JAI Press.

_____. 1991. "Ecovision: A Leadership Theory for Innovative Organizations." Organizational Dynamics 20: 50-62.

_____. 1990. "Involving Students in Decision-Making Can Reduce Conflict." Virginia Journal of Education June: 16-17.

_____. 1989. "Assessing Organizational Change: Quality of Work Life Interventions and the United States Postal Service. Ph.D. diss., Virginia Polytechnic Institute and State University.

Sorrell, Constance and Lewis, Joseph. 1998. "VDOT is Moving in a New Direction." Virginia Department of Transportation Publication: 1-19.

Starling, George. 1986. Managing the Public Sector (3rd). Chicago: The Dorsey Press.

Sowell, Thomas. 1995. The Vision of the Annointed: Self-Congratulations as a Basis for Social Policy. New York: Basic Books.

Terry, Larry. 1995. Leadership in Public Bureaucracies: The Administrator as Conservator. Thousand Oaks: Sage Publications.

Thurow, Lester. 1996. The Future of Capitalism: How Today's Economic Forces Shape Tomorrow's World. New York: William Morrow.

_____. 1980. The Zero-Sum Society. New York: Penguin Books.

Tichy, Noel and Ulrich, David. 1984. "The Leadership Challenge - A Call for the Transformational Leader." Sloan Management Review 25: 58-68.

USA Today Editorial Page, 7 March 2000, "Good Teachers Deserve Bonus," A16.

United States Postal Service. 1997. "Economic Value Added Financial Management and Pay for Performance Handbook F-6": 1-50.

Van Der Nerf, Martin. "How the University of Pennsylvania Learned that Outsourcing is no Panacea," The Chronicle of Higher Education, 7 April 2000, A39.

Walton, Richard and Schlesinger, Leon. 1979. "Do Supervisors Thrive in Participative Work Systems?" Organizational Dynamics 8: 25-38.

Wamsley, Gary, Goodsell, Charles, Rohr, John, Stivers, Camilla, and Wolf, James. "The Public Administration and Governance Process: Reinforcing the American Dialogue." In A Centennial History of the American Administrative State," edited by Ralph Chandler, 291-317. New York: MacMillian.

Wamsley, Gary and Zald, Mayer. 1973. The Political Economy of Public Organizations. Lexington, MA: Lexington Books.

Warwick, Donald. 1975. A Theory of Public Bureaucracy: Politics, Personality, and Organization in the State Department. Cambridge: Harvard University Press.

Webber, Alan. 1991. "Crime and Management: An Interview with New York City Police Commissioner Lee A. Brown." Harvard Business Review 69: 111-126.

Weick, Karl. 1996. "Prepare Your Organizations to Fight Fires." Harvard Business Review 74: 143-148.

_____. 1995. Sensemaking in Organizations. Thousand Oaks: Sage Publications.

Wilson, James. 1989. Bureaucracy: What Government Agencies Do and Why They Do It. New York: Basic Books.

The Winter Commission- Hard Truths/Tough Choices: An Agenda for State and Local Reform. 1993. Albany: The Nelson A. Rockefellow Institute of Government-State University of New York.

AUTHOR INDEX

SUBJECT INDEX

indirect benefits, 25, 28

Industrial Democracy, XII, XIII

lifetime employability, VII

lifetime employment, VII

managerial resistance to change, 31

New Pay, V, X, 1; defined, 2, 3; strategic goal, 4; where to start, XIV. *See also* variable pay

New Pay and Organization Learning: clear line-of-sight and learning, 69; design and alignment issues, 67, 68; double-loop learning, 63; leadership modeling, 64; learning and business education, 65; learning and skills acquisition, 65; organization fit, 63, 67; rewarded modeling, 64; single-loop learning, 63; training and learning, 66; Total Quality Management, 66; value-added learning, 69; vicarious learning, 64, 68

Organization Theory/Design, XII, 3, 4, 20

organization framebending, 19

political culture, 29

"private is better", V, 43. *See also* privatization

private sector organizations: parallel structures, XII, 51. *See also* Public Sector Change

privatization, 71, 72, 73; punctuated equilibrium, 72; school vouchers, 72; union members, 73; uniqueness of public organizations, 74

Public Administration and the Business Press: altruistic democracy, 57, 58, 59, 60; antideterministic leaders, 53, 54, 55, 59, 60; circles of causality, 60; deterministic leaders, 55, 56; determinism and Public Administration, 56, 57; image (re)constructions 55, 60; media feeding frenzy, 61; ongoing sensemaking, 54, 59; romance of leadership notion, 54. *See also* antideterminism

Public Administration: legal/political environment, 10; values, 6, 10

Public Management paradigm, XI